2015

Home
318 Lake View Dr
Washington MO 63090

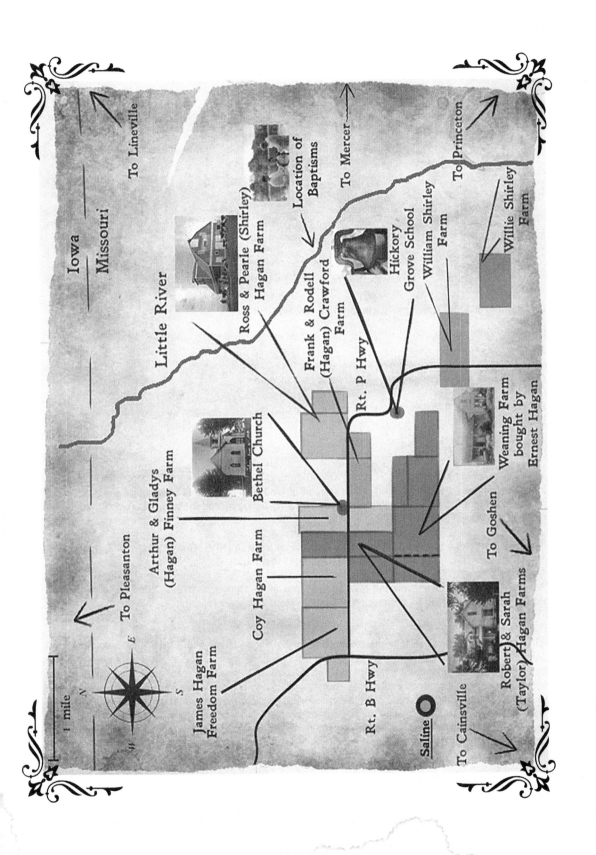

Copyright © 2014 by Raymond D. Hagan with Janice H. Wood

My First One Hundred Years
by Raymond D. Hagan with Janice H. Wood
Cover Design: Andrew Augspurger with Janice Hagan Wood

Printed in the United States of America
Edited by Xulon Press

All rights reserved solely by the authors. The authors guarantee all contents are original and do not infringe upon the legal rights of any other person or work. No part of this book may be reproduced in any form without the permission of the authors. The views expressed in this book are not necessarily those of the publisher.

Scripture.quotations taken from the New International Version (NIV). Copyright © 1973, 1978, 1984, 2011 by Biblica, Inc.™. Used by permission. All rights reserved.

Scripture.quotations taken from the New Living Translation. Copyright ©1996, 2004, 2007 by Tyndale House Foundation. Used by permission of Tyndale House Publishers, Inc.

Disclaimer:
All photographs in the book and appendix are from the Hagan family/authors' collection and used with permission. Memory is subjective; the authors' recollections may not be as others remember. Time brings change and consequently the authors and the publisher cannot be responsible for errors that may occur. The authors have tried to recreate events, locales and conversations from his memories of them, with no intention to cause hurt or harm to anyone. Although the authors and publisher have made every effort to ensure that the information in this book was correct and factual, the authors and publisher do not assume and hereby disclaim any liability to any party for any loss, damage, or disruption caused by errors or omissions, whether such errors or omissions result from negligence, accident, or any other cause.

A portion of this book was originally published by Xulon Press in 2012 under the title "Living Forever: Believing In What You Cannot See".

For information contact:
The Believer's Ministry
jimjanicewood@msn.com

My First ONE HUNDRED YEARS

Praying, Aiming High and Staying Focused

By
Raymond D. Hagan

with
Janice H. Wood

DEDICATION

I dedicate this book to my family. I love you one and all. I pray sharing my lifelong faith walk will help you trust God in every situation in your lives. I have tried to live in a way that will bring honor to our family name and to Jesus, by refusing opportunities that lead away from God. My greatest goal has always been to please the Lord first. I do this by praying, aiming high and staying focused on the direction He gives me. Everything else seems to fall into place after that. I pray this book will be a blessing to you.

INTRODUCTION

As I reflect on my father's memories, I see a well-lived life full of excitement. I am amazed at what he accomplished through the opportunities given to him. I love the overcomer's spirit that caused him to rise from unrelenting poverty, illness and injuries to achieve his dreams. The influence that guided him through an amazing set of parents was God-given and provided a solid Christian upbringing. Their gentle encouragement provided fertile soil for a Depression Era country boy to take on the world. I have watched a man of integrity, through sorrow and success, give thanks to God for everything, every day of his life. He continues to meet life head-on, with a great sense of humor and an optimistic faith in God. As you read memories of his life spanning a century, you will understand that he sets a high standard for living life to the fullest. What a blessing to be born into this family, to be raised by this godly man.
Janice Hagan Wood

ACKNOWLEDGEMENTS

It would be impossible to write a book like this without the assistance of my Lord Jesus Christ. He alone gave me life and guided me through every day I have lived. To Him I entrust this book. I am also grateful to my wonderful family and friends, whose lives have given me many stories to tell. Some are full of humor and others, sadness, but all combine to make the memories of my life. For kind and loving help along the way, I give special accolades to: Beth Wright, Naomi Orr, Hannah Alexander, Janie Beasley, Donna Hagan Covey, Garnet Hagan Gilmore and Robert Gilmore. I give my appreciation to everyone who helped make my vision of this book become reality.

TABLE OF CONTENTS

1. Beginning roots 15
2. Growing little Hagans 26
3. Pass the honey, Honey. 39
4. A hickory stick at Hickory Grove School 42
5. Celebrating Christmas country style 48
6. Living the country life. 51
7. Ohhh, Mama's cookin'! 58
8. Growing up Hagan 63
9. The influence that guided me .67
10. Family ties. 70
11. Moose money 82
12. The winds of change 85
13. Being an optimist, no matter what 90
14. The impossible dream 104
15. The day I died 113
16. Life after my death 120
17. The unexpected 127
18. Inspiring others to excellence 134
19. One + One = One 145
20. I'm in the Army now! Army Air Force, that is 152
21. The rest of my story 162

Appendix. 180

Chapter 1
BEGINNING ROOTS

It's truly amazing that I am here to share this story with you. I am not as old as Methuselah, even though it sometimes seems I've lived that long. Since you don't know me yet, allow me to introduce myself; my name is Ray. To be specific, I am Raymond Dale Hagan. I have lived a life vastly different from yours. I know this because I am part of a generation that grew up in a unique time in history; the economic, political, cultural, and even military turmoil is unprecedented. You will understand, as my story unfolds, these unique times created a group of people that are, by necessity, overcomers. I believe I grew up in the best century and in the best location possible. My generation lived through two world wars, the Great Depression, and a technological explosion that took us from horseback to space travel. Sadly, few members of my generation remain standing.

My family seems to think I have lived a life of excitement that others might be interested in reading, and so here I am, recording memories about my first 100 years, for future generations to read. I decided to start at the beginning, as far back as my memories will take me. I hope you enjoy the ride as we drive down memory lane together.

I have vivid memories of my grandfather, Robert William Hagan. When I was a youngster living in his home, Granddad Robert recounted his experiences about coming to Missouri. I loved to hear stories about his youth. I was captivated by his words, gestures and facial expressions as he told us stories about his adventures while he sat in his rocking chair after dinner. Granddad was a storyteller beyond compare. He was enthusiastic and sometimes quite loud as he told his tales. The thing that held all the children spellbound was the fact these were not made-up stories, but were actually true. My favorite story was how he came to live in beautiful Missouri. He carefully pondered his decision to move west from

Pennsylvania. As he made plans to move, he researched several possibilities and made a plan of action. This is how Granddad Robert told his story.

Robert had been awake all night. He stared at the ceiling, while the clock slowly ticked away the time. He reminisced about his life. He was twenty-one years old, and had lived in his parents' home in Clarion County, near Tylersberg, Pennsylvania, his entire life. He had attended the local school, excelling in mathematics. His father, Samuel passed away when he was just four years old. Samuel had been a farmer and logger. One day while rafting logs down the Alleghany River to Pittsburgh, Pennsylvania, he fell into the river. He was able to save himself, but due to this soaking, he developed pneumonia and passed away in September 1851, at the age of forty. He was buried on their farm in the Hagan cemetery, near the Hagan Church.

There were eight children in the family, but only six survived to adulthood. Robert's mother, Elisabeth struggled to raise them without a father. Robert and his brothers and sisters worked alongside their mother to keep food on the table and the farm property maintained. Only Robert and his brothers, John Henry and Jacob, remained in Pennsylvania with their mother. John Henry was like a father to Robert. Robert admired his oldest brother and respected the way he handled responsibilities for their mother. John Henry was married and had a little boy named Charles. The family jokingly called Charles "Shadow," because he followed Robert everywhere he went, sometimes riding on Robert's shoulders. The two loved each other and were rarely apart.

Elisabeth was discouraged. It had taken nearly seventeen years to settle her husband's estate. Finally her oldest son, John Henry filed a partition petition in 1867, seeking the Clarion County Court's permission to appraise the estate and sell the 138-acre farm. The appraised value was $2,700. It was sold for that amount to Elisabeth's daughter, Belinda and her husband, Christopher Frank, of Polk County, Iowa. John Henry promptly purchased the farm from Belinda. The estate was evenly divided among the living children and a widow's share for Elisabeth. Each child, including Robert, received $286.27. Elisabeth's widow's share of the estate was $858.82.

Today, Robert was going to leave everything he knew behind and start a life of his own. This was the last night in his parent's house, the Samuel and Elisabeth Hagan home, the last night in his bed, the last night he would enjoy the comforts of the only home he had known. Hardest of all was leaving little Charles behind. He had tried to explain to Charles why he was leaving. Charles was inconsolable. Robert vowed he would see this little boy again one day. He also realized this was going to be the most exciting day of his life.

Before dawn, he dressed in the dark. He already had his bag packed and quickly made a bed roll. He pulled on his boots and ran down the steps to eat his mother's hot biscuits. She was sad as she kissed her son good-bye. He told his mother and brothers he would write to them when he arrived at his destination.

Robert took his rifle, a few earthly belongings, some food and all the money he had, including his inheritance, and ran out the door. He had been able to find other people not far from his home with similar dreams to leave Pennsylvania and head west.

He was excited that he was going to meet a wagon train heading to Des Moines, Iowa. His wagon train was leaving from a town a day's journey north of the Hagan farm.

Everyone joining the wagon train was enthusiastic about their adventure. There were all sorts of people; families with children, young couples and a few elderly people as well. Most of them had wagons loaded with furniture, special treasures and household and farming implements. Robert's treasure was a head full of dreams about an amazing place called Missouri. He had been told it had gently rolling hills and miles and miles of rich and fertile farmland. It was green and lush with large trees. Berries grew wild, and there were many animals, such as deer, rabbits, squirrels, turkeys, and possibly bears. He could not wait to find out if these glowing reports about Missouri were true. His sisters, Sarah and Belinda, had written letters that convinced him this was the place where he could succeed in life. They promised to help Robert get established in this land of promise.

The 1,076 miles to Des Moines, Iowa was a very slow journey. The horses plodded along with their heavy loads. Robert walked much of the time. His outgoing personality helped him make friends with the other adventurers. He offered assistance when needed and would catch a ride on the wagons when he was able. On good days, the caravan would travel ten to fifteen miles. On rainy and muddy days, they might travel one mile. All able-bodied men worked hard to keep the animals and wagons going through slippery mud and rough terrain. The trip took nearly four months at this slow but steady pace.

The wagon train arrived in Des Moines, Iowa in the fall of 1868. All of the adventurers left behind everything they had known. Some continued westward with the wagon train, but Robert had other plans. As previously arranged, Robert went to the home of his older sister, Belinda and her husband, Christopher Frank, located nearby in Polk County, Webster Township in Iowa. After a brief visit with his relatives, Robert continued on the last part of his journey. He began walking to North Central Missouri. His final destination was Mercer County, just eighty-three miles south. The trees were turning beautiful colors and the nights were getting cool. He hoped to make it to his sister Sarah and husband, Ambrose Butler's house before the first snowfall. Robert ate what he hunted and cookies supplied by his sister Belinda, and slept on the hard, cold ground.

When Robert finally arrived in Missouri, he stayed with Sarah and Ambrose the first winter. They lived on a rented farm a few miles south of Iowa in Mercer County, Missouri. He helped them with their farming chores, and watched for opportunities to purchase or lease land for farming. This gave him a wonderful opportunity to learn about this beautiful area and time to plan for his future. When Sarah and Ambrose moved on, Robert rented the farm they were living on. He attended Bethel Church with his family and made new friends there. Robert wrote to his mother and brother Jacob, encouraging them to come to Missouri. He had a place prepared for them to start their new lives.

Robert's mother, Elisabeth and his younger brother, Jacob, moved to Missouri in 1869, one year after Robert arrived. The family had specifically planned for Elisabeth to travel with her son Jacob, rather than alone. This was to be sure she was well protected. Jacob was kindhearted and very close to his mother. He was a hard worker like his brother Robert, but shy and slow to develop friendships, due to a severe speech problem. Because of his intelligence and fine character, he was successful. In 1872, he married a local lady he met at Bethel Church, Hira Yetter. Her father, Hiram Yetter served in Bethel Church. Jacob purchased a 200-acre farm from the George Dunn family in 1875. He was acquainted with the Dunns because they also attended Bethel Church. Jacob paid $440 for the farm. A well-built house with a picket fence sat on his new property. His farm can be seen from the Bethel Church. It is located in Mercer County, Lindley Township, and one mile east of Bethel Methodist Church, off of rural Route P. Jacob became a prosperous farmer specializing in raising livestock, despite his stuttering problem. Jacob and Robert lived a few miles apart and attended Bethel Church together every Sunday. Jacob and Hira raised two sons and two daughters.

Jacob and Hira Hagan, and their four children, on the front porch of their home

Granddad Robert soon met a young lady with a similar Christian upbringing. They began courting with the permission of her parents, Reverend James and Eliza Snider Taylor. Like Robert, Sarah had been born in the eastern part of the nation, in Rockbridge County, Virginia. Her family first moved to Rockville, Indiana in 1860, and then to Mercer County Missouri in 1868. As a Christian, Sarah had a very strong faith and was the niece of a well-known street preacher and missionary to Africa and South America, Bishop William Taylor. Taylor University in Indiana is named in his honor. Sarah was greatly influenced by her Uncle William. She was devoted to Christ and made her life decisions according to biblical principles. Sarah had been raised on large farms. Being the oldest of nine children, Sarah knew how to successfully assist in every aspect of running a farm. Robert and Sarah were married August 23, 1870.

My grandparents, Robert and Sarah had a long and happy marriage. They were in agreement concerning life goals to make farming, faith and family their priorities. The first land they purchased in 1875 was the farm they were renting, and consisted of 180 acres. It is located two miles east of Saline, Missouri. They paid $3,800 to John and James Clark for this excellent land on a road now known as P highway. There was a historic barn on this farm when they purchased the property. The barn was built in the late 1850s, before the Civil War. It was used as a polling location during the Lincoln-Douglas presidential election, November 6, 1860. The barn is still known as the "Lincoln" barn. This treasure remains in the Hagan family today. Robert and Sarah's stately two-story white farmhouse was built a little later in 1907. Robert and Sarah raised an astonishingly large family on this farm. Thirteen children were born to them.

This hardworking couple was successful enough to have few money problems. In November of 1883, Robert and his father-in-law, James Taylor, purchased 400 acres from Charles Yates for $3,800. These four parcels of land were located directly behind Robert's home farm. Less than one year later in 1884, Robert purchased his father-in-law's interest in this land for $2,400, making Robert the sole owner. In 1891, Robert saw an opportunity to purchase excellent farmland across the road from his home farm. This property had road frontage on Route P. It consisted of three parcels of land totaling 222 acres. He was able to purchase this property for $4,330. This brought their property holdings to just over eight hundred acres of land.

Robert was well respected in the community. He was seated on the board of directors of several area banks, including the banks of Cainsville and Saline, both in Missouri, and the banks of Lineville and Pleasanton in the state of Iowa. Robert also served as a juror for trials involving fraud charges. He was a well-respected businessman and served in many community organizations.

Bethel Church has been the Hagan family church since 1866, when Robert's sister, Sarah and her husband, Ambrose Butler arrived in Missouri. It is located about sixteen miles northwest of Princeton on Route P, in Mercer County, and less than three miles south of the Iowa-Missouri line "as the crow flies." The church building was blown away in a storm on June 21, 1893 and rebuilt in the fall of 1894. It is still standing today. My granddad, Robert Hagan and his brother, Jacob Hagan helped rebuild the church, which is located between their farms on Route P. According to Bethel Church records, Robert and Sarah contributed the largest amount of any church member for the new building, and Robert also served on the building committee. This church has been a pillar of the community for 160 years. Today Bethel remains vital in this neighborhood and has continued to be the home church for the Hagan family down through the generations. Robert and Sarah were very active in this church and in many community activities. Through the years, Robert served as steward and trustee for Bethel Church. Sarah's uncle, Bishop William Taylor made three trips to Missouri to visit family. Each time he was there, he shared a message at Bethel Church. During one of his visits, in May of 1880, he held a baptismal service at the home of Robert and Sarah Hagan. He baptized several children, including Robert and Sarah's four oldest children; Jane (Eliza), Frank, Dell (Rodell) and Effie. Bishop Taylor recorded this. Sarah kept this note in her family Bible. What a blessing to be baptized by this great man.

My father, Ross Newton Hagan was born on May 5, 1885 in Mercer County, Missouri. He was the ninth child born to Robert and Sarah Hagan. He was named after two uncles, his mother's youngest brother, Ross Taylor and his mother's middle brother, Andrew Newton Taylor. In elementary school Ross developed a love of learning and a desire to pursue further education.

At that time, there was only an elementary school in the area. The closest high school was nine miles away in Pleasanton, Iowa. That is a long way on horseback. Dad rode his horse every day, to and from school until he completed the ninth grade. He never missed classes, even when it was snowing or freezing cold. Like his father and grandfather before him, he excelled in mathematics. Ross believed in the value of education and encouraged others to get all the schooling they could. Ross was known as a quiet man of great integrity, who did not fail to keep his word.

In the spring of 1902, Frank Hagan, the oldest son of Robert and Sarah, was badly hurt in an accident involving a horse during a spring storm. He was found unconscious with a life-threatening head injury. It was unknown if Frank was struck by lightning or if he was thrown off his horse. Frank did survive the trauma to his head, but was greatly affected by this. At the time of his accident, he owned 220 acres that he had purchased from his uncle, Archibald Taylor.

Frank, unable to care for his farm or business matters, moved back into his parents' home. Robert purchased Frank's farm, which adjoined his home farm, for $6,750. This money was used for Frank's care. Sadly, Frank passed away from illness in 1909 at age thirty. My grandparents and my father rarely spoke of this tragedy. I remember seeing pictures of Frank as a young man. He was a very handsome man with dark hair.

Hickory Grove School 1892
Ross is fifth child front row

Ross met a beautiful young lady named Pearle. Ethel Pearle Shirley was born December 4, 1884, in Mercer County, Missouri, the daughter of William Riley Shirley and Margaret Loretta Slover Shirley. She was a petite and beautiful lady. Her feet were so small she only wore size three shoes. Ross noticed that she was gentle, kind and compassionate. She demonstrated a strong faith in God and displayed a Christ-like demeanor. They began courting. Courting in that time meant learning about someone enough to know whether or not they are compatible for marriage. It involved friendship, discussing each individual's future plans, and getting to know each other's parents and siblings.

During the time they were courting, Pearl's father, William often told Ross stories about his family. William Shirley was an outstanding storyteller. Some of his stories were tall tales designed to make everyone laugh, but some related the history of his family. Ross learned that Pearle's family played an interesting part in history that was a source of pride in their family. The family had lived in Gentry County near Albany, Missouri since 1855. This is where Pearle's father, William Riley Shirley was born to Samuel and Mahala Shirley on November 28, 1857. However, this little family of three did not live there long due to unique circumstances.

There was great political unrest in the nation. Feelings were so strong that families were split apart. The presidential election had been heated and issues strongly debated. As 1861 ushered in the Civil War, even though the Samuel Shirley family was located close to Iowa, they were still in Missouri, which had many Southern sympathizers. There was great danger in Missouri for a man of strong Union allegiance, such as Pearl's grandfather, Samuel. This little family hastily moved back to Indiana. After settling his young family in Indiana, Samuel Shirley joined Company D of the 29th Indiana Infantry Regiment on September 21, 1864. He valiantly served in the Union army. Unfortunately, he contracted measles and other severe afflictions, which left him in poor health for the remainder of his life. Samuel was discharged at Chattanooga, Tennessee on May 15, 1865 at the age of twenty-eight.

Shortly after his return to Indiana in 1865, Samuel and Mahala returned to Putnam County, Missouri with their growing family of four children. After a few years they decided to uproot their family and move again. A combination of factors helped them to decide to move. Most important was Mahala's desire to be close to her family. She needed their help because of her husband's rapidly declining health. Even though he was quite ill, Samuel moved his family to Harrison Township, in Mercer County, Missouri, in 1872. The new Shirley homestead adjoined that of Mahala's parents, the Riley Williams homestead. Both are located east of Goshen, Missouri. By the time he moved his family to Mercer County, Samuel was very sick. He wintered in Waverly, Missouri to escape the extreme weather that so terribly worsened his condition. Sadly, Samuel Shirley died from tuberculosis on September 27, 1876. He was only thirty-nine years old. William Riley Shirley, their oldest son had to take over as head of the family in his father's stead. Throughout my life, I heard the story of my brave great-grandfather, told over and over by my grandfather, William Riley Shirley.

Ross grew fond of Pearle and her parents. William Shirley was an intelligent and happy man who often whistled and laughed easily. He loved a good joke and frequently played pranks to make everyone laugh. At the Shirley home there was music to go along with the laughter. Gertrude, Pearl's sister, played an organ that had to be pumped with foot pedals. Pearle played the piano and sang, and William Shirley played the harmonica. An evening in this home was always full of fun and popcorn too.

During this time of courtship, Ross and a few of his close friends rode the train to St. Louis. They were on an adventure to see the World's Fair. It was held in 1904 in honor of the centennial celebration called "Louisiana Purchase Exposition." This was the first train ride for all of the young men. Ross had his first ice cream cone at the fair. He loved it. He also saw many futuristic ideas from other states and nations. Much to the surprise of these country boys, the fair was a huge event. It sprawled over 1,200 acres. There were more than 1,500 buildings, connected by about seventy-five miles of roads and walkways. Today this area is known as Forrest Park and is located on the campus of Washington University.

The Palace of Agriculture alone covered almost twenty acres. This agriculture exhibit was the obvious favorite for Ross. He acquired ideas he later implemented in his farming career. The fair had a theme song, "Meet Me in St. Louis." It was a popular song for many years. I can remember hearing this song on the radio and people singing it around a piano during my early years, long after the fair was over.

Ross bought Pearle an elegant satin souvenir pillow with the words, "The St. Louis World's Fair" embroidered on it. Two edges of the pillow had golden fringe. She cherished it as the first gift Ross gave her. Pearle placed this pillow on a round, wooden rocking chair, where it remained for the rest of her life.

After four years of courtship, on Tuesday, September 3, 1907, Ross married Ethel Pearle Shirley in Cainsville, Missouri. The union was officiated by Rev. Lewis Weary. They spent the rest of their wedding day in Princeton, ate in a restaurant and returned home the same evening. Soon after, they took a wedding trip to Oklahoma by train. Pearle was extremely nervous about riding a train for the first time, and going so far away from home. Ross, on the other hand, was an experienced traveler by then and patiently calmed Pearle's fears. The honeymooners visited Will and Kitty Hagan and their two young sons. Will was the next older brother of Ross. Will and Kitty had homesteaded a farm near Watonga, Oklahoma.

Pearle, like her husband Ross, was a very hard worker, and both believed in strong family relationships. Another way they were similar was the way they treated others. They were courteous and slow to anger with each other and everyone around them. Ross was a quiet and soft-spoken man who, in my memory, never raised his voice to a child or an adult. These gentle people went out of their way to avoid hurting others. I never heard either of my parents say an unkind word about anyone. This type of unselfish conduct is called being a peacemaker in the Bible. Ross and Pearle shared a strong faith in Jesus, the Son of God. They also held strong political views. They proudly supported the Republican Party, as did their parents and grandparents. Pearle was not allowed to vote because she was a woman. Only men had voting privileges at that time.

Ross and Pearle rented a farm owned by his parents for the first few years of their marriage. My granddad, Robert Hagan laughingly called this "the weaning house," because many of his twelve children began their married lives there, before buying their own farms. This farm was later purchased by Dad's brother, my uncle Ernest Hagan. Ross joined his dad, Robert, to work several of his farms. They were "farmed on the shares." This meant Dad did the work on Granddad's land for a percent of the income. Several of my other uncles "farmed on the shares" as well, on Granddad's farms. In 1911, W.B. Rogers published a book "Rogers' Souvenir History of Mercer County Missouri." He included an article about granddad Robert indicating he owned a "nice farm of six hundred and eighty acres."

The Hagan Family
Children of Samuel Hagan (1811-1851) & Elisabeth Heasley Hagan (1814-1896)
John Henry Hagan (1836–1894)*
Angelina Hagan (1838–1855)*
Elizabeth Jane Hagan Shotts (1840–1911)*
Sarah Ann Hagan Butler (1842–1916)*
Catherine Ann Hagan (1842–1842)*
Belinda Eleanor Hagan Frank (1845–1912)*
Robert William Hagan (1847–1928)*
Jacob Nealy Hagan (1849–1925)*

Children of Robert Wm Hagan (1847-1928) & Sarah Taylor Hagan (1851-1923)
Eliza Jane Hagan Dunn (1871–1936)*
Frank Emory Hagan (1873–1909)*
Elizabeth Rodell Hagan Crawford (1874–1970)*
Effie May Hagan Rockey (1876–1953)*
Mirtis Loretta Hagan Mark (1877–1962)*
James Stuart Hagan (1879–1964)*
William Taylor Hagan (1881–1949)*
Infant Son Hagan (1884–1884)*
* Ross Newton Hagan (1885–1968)*
Fleety Beatrice Hagan Shirley (1887–1975)*
Ernest Clarence Hagan (1889–1978)*

Gladys Irma Hagan Finney (1891–1966)*
Coy Virgil Hagan (1894–1966)*

<u>The Shirley Family</u>
<u>Children of Samuel Shirley (1837-1876) & Mahala Williams Shirley Slover (1840-1911)</u>
    <u>*William Riley Shirley (1857–1939)*</u>
    Mary F. Shirley Larason (1860–1884)*
    Erastus Harvey Shirley (1862–1920)*
    Nancy Shirley (1865–____)*
    Lovey Alice Shirley Slover (1867–1907)*
    John Thomas Shirley (1870–1948)*
    Jemima Ellen Shirley (1873–1881)*
    Rosa E. Shirley (1875–1881)*
    Raleigh Daniel Slover (1882–1963)**

<u>Children of William R Shirley (1857–1939) & Margaret L. Slover Shirley (1858–1943)</u>
    Albert Bertam Shirley (1881–1907)*
    Lillian Blanche Shirley Woods (1882–1966)*
    <u>** Ethel Pearle Shirley Hagan (1884–1966)*</u>***
    Stella Maude Shirley (1887–1888)*
    Minnie May Shirley (1889–1889)*
    Grace Edith Shirley Swingle (1891–1985)*
    Elsie Gertrude Shirley (1894–1993)*
    William Glenn Shirley (1899–1972)*

Chapter 2

GROWING LITTLE HAGANS

During their stay in "the weaning house," Ross and Pearle had a beautiful blonde, blue-eyed daughter, Jessie Delores, born April 19, 1908, and a handsome dark-haired son, Albert Ross, born January 2, 1910.

In 1912, Ross and Pearle had the opportunity to purchase his uncle Jacob Hagan's nearby farm. Jacob was only sixty-two, but ready to retire from farming due to health problems. They did not hesitate. The young couple got a loan from the local bank for $12,256 to buy the farm and named it the Fairview Stock Farm.

Pearle was thankful the farm already had a well-maintained home on it. The house was built around the year 1860 by George and Martha Dunn. It had huge notched logs as the foundation, and was built with wooden pegs and square nails. The house was built with a beautiful front porch and a picket fence. The first floor had a parlor, kitchen, dining room, one bedroom and small nursery. The kitchen was equipped with a wood-burning cooking stove, cupboards, counters and a large table that served as a workstation. Upstairs were two additional bedrooms with sloping ceilings. The stairway was very steep and did not have a handrail. In the center of the home, on the first floor was a wood-burning heating stove. This was the only source of heat for the entire home in the winter. Pearle kept large cast iron teakettles of water on the stove, to help raise the humidity levels. Behind the house and down the hill was an outhouse, which was typical for this era. In this family, it was called the backhouse. On cold and stormy winter nights, chamber pots were used. Well water was pumped by hand and hauled to the house in buckets.

My parents happily welcomed a second baby boy to their family, Raycel Shirley Hagan, soon after moving to their new farm. Then a darling, dark-haired girl, Vee Marie Hagan, arrived shortly after Raycel. As his family grew, Ross added a room to the existing house and screened in the porch.

Their little family now had six places at the dinner table. Along with a growing family, Ross and Pearl had a thriving farming operation. Ross also farmed for his dad, Robert in his large farming business. Ross worked on his dad's farms as well as his own. Robert was getting older and slowing down considerably. He spent more time attending meetings at the various banks where he served as a board member. Ross and Robert remained in a close relationship all of their lives. Although they had different personalities (with Ross being softer spoken and easier going), they were simply the best of friends. The respect and absolute trust they displayed for each other was quite obvious.

Ross soon saw the need for a barn that would allow him to maximize his work on their new farm. Being talented in mathematics and building skills, he started to lay out design plans for a large, progressively designed barn. It thoughtfully included everything needed to raise cattle. He incorporated several innovations that are quite unique for this age of barn, including: a silo, two rooms to store corn and oats, and a large hayloft running the length of the barn, with feeding chutes on both sides to the stalls below. The hayloft (or second floor) of the barn was the size of a school gymnasium, and doubled as a basketball court in later years. The first floor of the barn held the stalls that were used for cattle and occasionally hogs. The large silo was filled with silage that was used in winter to feed sheep and cattle. Silage is ground-up green stalks or fodder that is compacted and stored in the silo to ferment. It is used as supplemental feed for cud-chewing animals. I remember the smell of the silage as we fed it to the cattle in winter; it had an interesting, fresh smell. When the silo was empty, it was possible to climb to the top of it from the inside.

Ross carefully planned every detail so precisely that each piece of lumber was cut before assembly was started. The barn was built using the finest materials available. When neighbors came to help raise the barn, it went together like a precision cut puzzle. This amazing barn was started in 1914 and finished in 1915. The barn was, in later years, one of the first in the region to have electricity wired into it.

When the barn was completed, Ross built two six-foot woven wire fences to direct the path of the livestock from the barn to the well, where we pumped water by hand for the livestock. This made caring for them more manageable, especially in bad weather. Dad would probably be surprised that a century later, his remarkable red barn remains a community landmark and still sits perfectly straight on the hilltop. The red barn can easily be seen at a distance from Bethel Church. My brother, Raycel took great care of this treasure his entire life. In 2010, it was voted the most beautiful barn in America by the popular magazine, "Living the Country Life." The editors had a difficult time narrowing down the hundreds of candidates to the six finalists. In the end, the winner was the Ross

Hagan barn near Mercer, Missouri. It is indeed beautiful and wonderfully built. When I gaze at this amazing structure, from the foundation to the top of the roof, I am most impressed that it was designed so perfectly without the assistance of an architect, and was built completely by hand without modern tools or electricity.

The smaller old barn was still required for the horses, and had pens for sheep and hogs, if needed. Both barns had cribs to store corn and oats.

The Ross Hagan Barn built in 1915.
The words above the painting are Fairview Stock Farm.

I was born March 5, 1915, at home on the farm. The big red barn and I are the same age. My mother said the day I was born we had the deepest snow she had ever seen. The drifts were blown up to the eves of the house and covered the tops of fences. Mom signaled Dad that she needed him, by lighting a coal oil lamp in the front parlor window. When Dad saw the light flickering through the snowflakes, he saddled two horses and hurried to the neighbor's house to bring back a lady to help Mom with my birth. A doctor was unable to get to our house because of the snow. The first time a doctor saw me was in April of that year. The snowstorm caused issues for more than just my family that March. The *Chillicothe Constitution*, in nearby Chillicothe, Missouri, printed this article on the snowstorm in the Friday, March 5, 1915 edition.

The Chillicothe Constitution.

CHILLICOTHE, MISSOURI, FRIDAY, MARCH 5, 1915.

SNOW COVERS THE STATE OF MISSOURI

NEBRASKA REPORTS DEPTHS OF SIXTEEN INCHES.

In the Joplin Mining District Work Has Been Stopped on Account of Swollen Streams.

(Special to The Constitution)
Kansas City, March 5.—The greater part of the state is covered with snow to the depth of one foot. In many places the snow is reported from twelve to fourteen inches deep. Around Joplin in the mining district the streams are swollen and work in the mines has been abandoned. The snow in that section was preceded by a rain and up until this morning the snow melted as fast as it fell. A rise of fifteen feet is reported in the Spring river near Joplin.

The state of Nebraska reports a 16 inch snowfall.

The storm is raging over the Great Lakes today and is traveling eastward.

The snow has caused a complete tie-up in the street car service in many of the larger cities. In Kansas City and St. Louis hundreds of men with shovels are trying to haul the snow away, but they are unable to keep the streets cleaned for traffic.

The heavy snow storm of Thursday and Friday is causing the trains entering Chillicothe from the east, south and west, to be late and it is anticipated they will be running later tonight. Trains from the west were more than an hour late at noon today.

Rural mail carriers out of Chillicothe and other offices in this vicinity experienced one of the hardest trips of the season yesterday. In many places drifts were encountered which made traveling hard.

Travel was as difficult yesterday as during some of the colder weather, but the carriers in nearly every instance stuck to their routes. There has not been a day this winter that they have not carried the mail.

Just fourteen months after I was born, my sister Reva Pearle was born. We were close in age and in relationship. During our early years I played with Reva and protected her. I clearly remember my mother telling me she was my baby and I was to watch out for her. I felt she was my responsibility my whole life. When we were very young, I would lead Reva around by her hand, everywhere I went. We now needed eight chairs around our dining table.

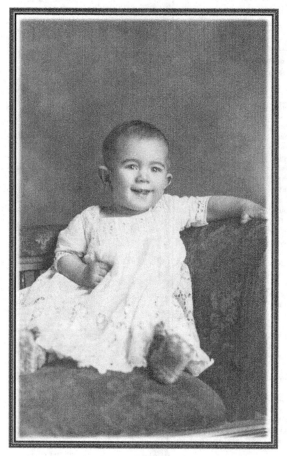

Raymond Dale Hagan; 1 year old

My first memory was when I was about two years old. I was sitting in a highchair at the dinner table with my brothers and sisters. The food looked so good. The older children were eating and talking. Fried chicken was passed around the table, but I did not get any. Mashed potatoes were passed and I did not get any of those either. I had no food and was so hungry. The smell of Mom's wonderful cooking was making the hunger worse. I decided I was going to get some dinner. Finally I said, "Pass the sorghum." Vee, my quiet older sister, had big beautiful eyes and usually noticed everything around her. She was very attentive to the needs of others. True to her character, Vee poured sorghum on my plate, but gave me no other food to go with it. I expected her to hand me a biscuit, as she would usually do. I was so upset about not having bread that I turned the plate upside-down on my head. Everyone laughed and said, "Look at Raymond!" Mom came running with a towel and cleaned me up. I did not get to eat that evening. I did remember all the attention I received! The next time I tried the sorghum trick, I got a spanking from my mother.

As a child, I loved to climb on anything around. When I was two-and-a-half years old, I crawled up a fence beside the old barn, which was located across the road from our house. I kept going up until I reached the peak of the barn.

That was a long way up. I had not thought about going back down. Mother saw me and called to me to get down. I told her I would if she would take my picture. I did not look down. Mom got the camera and took my picture. Then she quietly directed me down and off the barn. Years later I learned how much that frightened her. It is a good thing I selected the smaller barn to climb, rather than the new, much taller barn.

Little Ray climbing to the top of the old barn

Reva and I usually played together because we were so close in age. We were creative about making our own fun. We learned to walk on homemade stilts by watching our older brothers, and we loved to run races. Reva could run quite fast. We often played games like "tag" or hide-and-seek. We had very few toys that were store bought. Each of my sisters had a doll, and sometimes at Christmas we would get something small. When I was little, my favorite toy was a stuffed animal that looked like a baboon. One day while Reva and I were playing in the yard, an older man, a tramp, came walking by. For some reason, he took my toy and set it on fire in the ditch. We were very upset. We yelled at him and chased him down the road with a pitchfork, but sadly my wonderful toy was gone.

One sunny spring afternoon, Reva and I were playing in the old machine shed, looking at everything Dad had stored there. We opened a can of paint and it spilled all over Reva's dress. We were afraid to tell Mother, so we came up with a story that we were out in the field and Reva fell into a big hole. The paint was in the hole and got all over her dress. Mother wanted me to show her where the hole was, so I took her out toward the field and then told her I couldn't remember where it was. She knew the true story, but that was the end of it. I learned a lesson about honesty that day. One lie leads to another. I never wanted to tell another lie after that experience.

As part of a large extended family, we often had what we called "get-togethers." When I was three-and-a-half years old, there was a big family get-together at Uncle Rob Larason's place. My parents had to leave to attend another gathering. They asked my Aunt Grace Swingle to watch Reva and me. I went to Aunt Grace and said, "I'm hungry!" She kept saying, "It's okay, honey, I'll get you something in a little bit." I was so hungry that I left and walked back home, a distance of about two-and-a-half miles down a crooked dirt road. I remember stopping at a fork in the road to consider which way to go. I almost took a wrong turn toward Little River. I walked up a hill and could see our house ahead. When I got home, I went inside to find there were leftover eggs and sausage from our breakfast, in the middle of the table, covered by a clean white towel. I ate a few cold fried eggs. After my belly was full, I felt tired and laid down on Mom and Dad's bed. Before long, I heard something and peeked out the window. There were two men from the family get-together in the driveway. They went out to the barn and looked around, then came back to the house and knocked on the door. I hid under the bed. When they finally left, I went to sleep on the bed again. A little later I heard someone knocking on the door. I peeked out the window. I recognized my uncle, so I opened the door. He came to take me back to the family dinner. This time we went in a car. When my parents came back, they were told what I had done. I was afraid I was going to be in trouble, but they never said anything to me.

When my oldest brother, Albert was in the fifth grade, I would have been four years old. I always considered Albert to be an example of a very good boy. Albert was quiet and polite like my father, but looked like my mother. He did well in school. He surprised me by getting into trouble one day. I always thought he was Mom's favorite and never got into mischief, until that day. He came home from school with a note. My mother and Albert were in the kitchen discussing the contents of the note. She became upset with Albert. He bolted out the back door and into the yard to run away from her. She grabbed a long switch and ran after him. Albert quickly climbed up a tree and went out on a limb. He was cornered! Mom reached up into the tree and switched his legs. It must have smarted because he yelled out for her to stop, which she did immediately. I think that was the only switching he ever received. I know I tried to be well behaved the rest of the day. However, not long afterwards, I got into trouble too.

One evening we had company. I was sitting on the floor, listening to Dad and another man talk about a war in a far-away place. They had read about the war in the newspaper. They were quite concerned because it was a very big war. I sat quietly, trying to figure out what a war might be. Years later I understood what they were discussing. In 1917, the United States entered World War I. The farmers, as well as all Missourians, experienced a wartime economy. For farmers, the change was significant. Since 1914, Midwestern farmers had experienced economic prosperity. Along with farmers everywhere, they were urged to be patriotic by increasing their production. Farmers purchased more land and raised more corn, beef, and pork, for the war effort. It seemed that no one could lose, as farmers expanded their operations, made more money, and at the same time, helped the Allied war effort. After the war, Missouri farmers soon saw wartime farm subsidies eliminated. Beginning in 1920, many farmers had difficulty making the payments for debts they had incurred during the war. This was the important subject my dad and his friend were discussing that day.

Jessie, my blue-eyed blonde sister, was very pretty and quite a tease. While I sat near my father she walked past me, barefooted as usual. She reached over and stuck her toe in my mouth. I ran after her into the kitchen. We ran around and around through the rooms until Dad reached over and thumped me on the head. Down I went! It hurt pretty badly. As far as I know, he never touched me, or any of the other children, any other time. I felt a little humiliated, but tried to sit more quietly as the men talked. This incident helped me remember this important conversation.

In spite of having so many children, discipline was rarely needed in the Hagan house. For the most part we all worked hard and tried to mind our parents. Of course, we could get boisterous, especially Raycel and me. Occasionally, my mother would grab a tea towel and gently snap us when we got too rowdy. She often got tickled and laughed with us. It was difficult for my parents to keep up with seven active youngsters and work two large farms.

In 1919, Dad, being a master carpenter, built a garage with a workshop, where he could park his car. We owned one of the first new cars in our area. It was an exciting day when he came home with a black 1919 Model T Ford he purchased for $375. It had a hand crank in the front that we had to turn to start the car. Even though I was quite young, this was the most exciting thing to happen in my life. I loved to ride in that car and feel the wind in my face. The children all clamored to get a ride in it. Not everyone liked those first automobiles. One day we were coming home in Dad's car when we came upon a buggy that was pulled by two horses. The custom was for the buggy to pull over to the right so that the faster car could pass. The buggy driver did just the opposite, blocking the way so that we could not pass. We had to follow him many miles. People, who did not own cars, could be quite stubborn about yielding the right of way. There were no paved roads in the country, so they could get covered by dust from the dirt roads. The roads that did exist were rough and slippery in bad weather. I saw my dad and other men drive through pastures more than once just to avoid the bad roads.

Winter weather in North Missouri can be very cold with frequent snow and sometimes ice storms. I remember a significant ice storm when I was almost five years old. My older brothers, Raycel and Albert were sledding. The best sledding hill was next to the road in a pasture. Three strands of barbed wire were strung across a gap in the fence. This barbed wire served as a gate. While sledding down the hill, they had to duck their heads to get under the barbed-wire fence. I wanted to take a turn on the sled, but they said no. They didn't think I could duck my head to get under the barbed wire. I convinced them that I could, so they let me take a turn. On my first ride down the hill, I didn't wait to duck until I got to the fence. I ducked my head as soon as they pushed me. Then I remembered I didn't have to duck until I reached the barbed wire. I raised my head just in time to get caught on the wire. I stopped instantly, but the sled kept going on down the hill without me. It took a moment to realize my head was caught on the barbed-wire fence. There were two long slices across the top of my head, which caused blood to run down my face, into my eyes, and mouth. We seldom went to the doctor, so Albert and Raycel ran me home to Mom for treatment. The scars were permanent.

My grandparents, Robert and Sarah were beginning to slow down with their increasing age, and decided to sell some of their farm land to their children. They sold one farm, located across Route P from their home farm, to their son Coy for $16,000. Near the same time they sold another property to their son, Jim Hagan for $4,250, and another small property to their son, Will Hagan for $500 and services rendered. In this way they had money to live on in retirement, but most importantly, because they sold only to their children, this kept their family closely connected to one another. Their priorities of faith, family and farming were passed forward through the generations due to their careful planning. This affected my life directly because I grew up surrounded by many cousins, aunts and uncles. We went to the same schools, church and family functions. Everywhere I went, I was surrounded by Hagans who loved me, encouraged me, and kept me safe. There was always someone to reach out to in time of need. This wonderful and unique atmosphere provided fertile soil for a country boy to grow up confident and secure.

During the spring of 1920, my granddad Robert Hagan went on a train trip with his daughter and son-in-law, my Uncle John and Aunt Effie Rockey. It was a long trip and some of the family did not think Granddad should try to go due to his age. Aunt Ef said she would make sure he was well cared for. They left Missouri and went to Clarion County, Pennsylvania, to see the original Hagan home place. They visited the house Granddad was born and raised in, and the spring on that property. Granddad Robert remembered the old mill in Oil City, where he had taken wheat and corn for grinding when he was a child. Aunt Ef took pictures of her father beside the house, the Hagan family church where the whole family attended services, and next to his father Samuel's marker in the Hagan cemetery. In spite of the family's concerns, they made it home safely with many pictures and stories to share.

The Hagan Family House in Clarion County, Pennsylvania

The Hagan Family Church in Clarion County, Pennsylvania

August 22, 1920, we went to the largest celebration I had ever attended. It was my grandparents Robert and Sarah Hagan's fiftieth anniversary party. It was held at their beautiful large two-story white house. There were so many people in attendance, I was overwhelmed; I could not get away from them. One hundred thirty-four family members and friends filled the house, yard, and all of the porches. The old Lincoln barn was even full of people. I knew my other grandparents, the Shirleys, were there, but I could not find them in the crowd. Photographers took pictures of different groups of people. I did not appear in any of the pictures, because I ran away and hid. People were dressed up in suits and ties, hats and fancy dresses. Mother made sure each of her children wore freshly ironed dress-up clothing. My sisters had their hair curled and tied with ribbons. A wonderful meal was served. The tables had white tablecloths and extended across the entire front lawn. Even this was not enough seating. People were eating everywhere; on blankets on the ground, standing up, leaning on the house and against trees. Raycel and I hid under the serving tables set up in the dining room, grabbed something to eat, and ran as far away from the crowd as possible. My grandparents were given several presents and a special cake. Granddad received a gold fountain pen and a beautiful cane with a gold handle. My grandmother received a gold ring and a large umbrella with a gold handle. I have no idea why I felt the need to run from the crowd, but I can still feel the panic that filled my heart that day.

Fifty years of marriage celebrated at the Robert and Sarah Hagan home.
Their lovely house was built in 1907.

Ordinarily my family and I loved to go to Grandma and Granddad's house, especially for dinner. She was a marvelous cook, so when she asked us to come for a meal, I could not wait to get there. I was usually the first one to wash my hands and run to her dinner table, with Raycel right behind me. Memories of her cream gravy still make my mouth water. She made sure we thanked the Lord for our food before we began to eat. She thanked the Lord often, for all things that were good in her life, at mealtime and throughout the day.

Just after Christmas that winter, when I was five years old, my youngest brother Darrell was born. He was the seventh and final child born to my parents. It had been several years since their last baby was born, so everyone, including grandparents, was thrilled. He was named William Robert Darrell, to satisfy both grandfathers. It goes without saying, he was greatly loved and spoiled by everyone. We now needed a larger dining table to accommodate nine chairs.

<u>Ross and Pearle (Shirley) Hagan's Children:</u>
Jessie Deloris, born April 19, 1908
Albert Ross, born January 2, 1910
Raycel Shirley, born December 17, 1911
Vee Marie, born January 27, 1913
<u>*Raymond Dale, born March 5, 1915*</u>
Reva Pearle, born May 12, 1916
William Robert Darrell, born January 21, 1921

134 GUESTS CELEBRATE A GOLDEN WEDDING

Mr. and Mrs. Robert Hagan Live on Farm Near Saline Where They Settled After Marriage Fifty Years Ago.

On Sunday, August 22, Mr. and Mrs. Robert Hagan, well known and prominent residents of Lindley township, celebrated their golden wedding anniversary. A great feast was served on a table that extended across the front lawn, and around this gathered one hundred and thirty-four relatives and friends. It was truly a merry gathering.

Mr. Hagan, who is 72 years old, was born in Pennsylvania, and came to Mercer county in 1867. Mrs. Hagan is 69 years old. She was born in West Virginia and came here in 1866. 1, August, 1870 they were married and settled on a farm two miles east of Saline. And their fifty years of happy married life has been spent on that farm. Eleven of their children are now living, and all were present at the celebration except Mrs. Wiley Dunn of Abbyville, Kansas. Besides these, 33 grand children and 4 great grand children were numbered among the guests.

After the anniversary dinner that day, Billy Mullinix of Linn, in behalf of the children, presented Mrs. Hagan with a gold ring and gold headed umbrella, and Mr. Hagan with a gold fountain pen and a gold headed cane. Then Mrs. Hagan gave each one of her daughters... Mrs. Hagan...

Dave Robbins and children, Mr. and Mrs. W. O. Mullinix, Ben L. Mark, and daughter Emma, Fred Williams, John Robbins and children, Albert Dorland and children, Billie Kirkpatrick and daughters Mary, Archie Kirkpatrick and daughter Silvia, Dorothy Booth, Mr. and Mrs. Barnhizer and three children, Willis Houk, Mr. and Mrs. G. A. Crawford and two children, Mr. and Mrs. ... Seymour, Iowa. Mitchell of ... and Mr... Mrs. ... and ... M...

Robert & Sarah Hagan
50th Anniversary

Ross Hagan leaning on tree

Chapter 3

PASS THE HONEY, HONEY

Two people were very important to me as I grew up: my mother's parents, my grandparents, William Riley Shirley and Margaret Slover Shirley. Their children were Albert, Blanche, Grace, Ethel Pearle (my mother), Gertrude, and Willy. My oldest brother was named after their son Albert, who passed away from spinal meningitis at the age of twenty-six.

Many times I would go to their house to spend the night. I thought it was wonderful they owned two hunting dogs. Grandfather would take me hunting when I was too small to even carry a gun. We would use oil lanterns at night, take the two hunting dogs and hunt small varmints like civet cats, skunks, raccoons, and opossums. The two dogs would tree something and then we would either shoot it, or scare it out of the tree so the dogs would chase it. Granddad Shirley always had something fun for us to do when we visited.

My Uncle Willy and Aunt Zelma Shirley gave me a small rifle when I was just six years old. This was very young to own a gun, but Granddad Shirley took the time to teach me about gun safety and care. I will always remember those lessons. I tried to be safe and trustworthy with my gun and used it for many years. It was a little 22, single shot Hamilton rifle. I would hunt with my dad, Granddad Shirley, and Uncle Willy Shirley. We would eat the rabbits and squirrels we hunted.

One summer night, Grandma Shirley cooked dinner for a large group of relatives and friends. Some of the people who came were Uncle Willy and Aunt Zelma Shirley, Morris Swingle, Oscar Wood, Gertrude Shirley, my sisters, and older brothers, Albert and Raycel. I was the youngest one attending by several years. After dinner, the adults lingered at the table enjoying fresh peach pie. Granddad Shirley began telling about a terrible problem he was having with rats in his corn crib. The men gave him ideas on the best way to get rid of the rats. Granddad suggested we go on a rat hunt. Along with a great deal of discussion and laughter, a plan was devised. All of the men were to take part, including my brothers and me. Granddad stationed each of the men evenly around the corn crib, including Albert, Raycel and me. We were armed with a stick or club to use as a weapon. The plan was to scare the rats so badly they would flee the corn crib. We were to club the rats as they ran past us. The person with the most rats would be declared the winner of the contest. I was placed in the back of the crib, next to Granddad Shirley. The men began to make noise, beating the side of the wooden crib. Right on cue, the rats began scurrying out of the corn crib. Everyone tried their best to get the rats. I was able to get only one. Granddad had a huge pile of twenty. Then he said, "Count how many you were able to get." After everyone had counted, he said, "Well, look at Raymond. He has twenty-one!" and pointed to his pile. "Raymond is the winner!" No one was more surprised than me. Granddad laughed and patted me on the back for doing a fine job. No wonder I loved to go to the Shirley home.

One morning, Reva and I were summoned to our Shirley grandparents' farm. We could not imagine what they wanted us to do. When we got there, they explained they had a special surprise for us. Reva and I followed them into the barnyard. We saw an amazing number of squealing piglets. They had been recently weaned. While Granddad was feeding them, he told Reva and me to pick one out and we could have it. We looked them over carefully. Finally we picked one. Granddad laughed and said we picked the very best one. Then he tied the piglet's legs together and put it in his car. He drove all three of us home. On the way home, he explained that we needed to be sure the little pig had water and food and was watched carefully. Reva and I raised that pig until it got big enough to run with Dad's hogs. We eventually sold it for $24 and put the money in the bank. Reva and I learned several life lessons about responsibility, banks and money.

Grandma Shirley was a gentle and intelligent lady. She had been a teacher before she married. I learned from Albert and Jessie that if I ever needed help with homework, Grandma Shirley was the best person to ask. I remember her having a sweet smile, being quiet and well spoken. She quietly put the needs of others before her own. My mother and sister Vee were much the same. My grandfather would often say his wife was the best-looking woman in the county and the most intelligent. He loved her with a tender love. Near the end of every meal, he would look at her, smile, and say, "Pass the honey, Honey."

In the spring of 1923, my grandmother, Sarah Taylor Hagan, the first person I knew well, passed away. I was surprised and hurt that she would leave my granddad. She was seventy-one years old, which seemed old to me. At that time, teenagers also seemed old to me. Her passing brought new ideas and experiences into my sheltered existence. I learned what it meant to grieve. I saw adults cry openly. I saw my Grandfather Hagan, a stable and solid man, visibly shaken. I attended my first funeral. Most people wore black dress-up clothes. Some had black armbands. The thing that shook me the most was the fact that people needed to be buried. That was a very troubling thought to me. I saw men digging the grave in Bethel Cemetery. I was told she was in heaven and that she was an angel. I pondered this idea. Where was heaven? What was it like? Vee told me I asked too many questions and that heaven was up in the sky. If heaven was up in the sky, why had they buried her in the ground? I had a lot of thoughts to contemplate. Over the next few months, I realized that because my grandmother was in heaven, many things were changing here on earth.

Chapter 4
A HICKORY STICK AT HICKORY GROVE SCHOOL

About the time I started grade school, modern technology hit our little community in a life-changing way. A long-awaited telephone line was set up along our country roads. When we were finally connected to the line, Dad bought a rather large wooden box and mounted it on the wall near the kitchen. We could pick up the receiver, place it on our ear, and talk into the attached speaker. It was amazing to hear others speak plainly when they were many miles away.

Hickory Grove was the grade school my family attended, from first through eighth grade. This included both of my parents, all of my siblings and many aunts, uncles and cousins. It was located south of our farm. The structure was a small, one-room schoolhouse with outhouses in the back yard. Inside were rows of small desks. Each student had their own desk with a chair attached. A chalkboard was in front of the classroom, near the teacher's desk. There was a long backless bench in the front of the classroom. When the teacher was presenting something grade specific, the students in that grade would go to the front of the room and sit on that uncomfortable bench. The remaining students would sit at their desks to work on assignments independently. It was difficult to concentrate with a noisy class so close. Usually, there were several students talking while the teacher asked questions. In the middle of one wall was a large wood-burning heating stove. If you sat close to this stove, you would get too hot, but if you sat far away from the stove, you would get very cold. It seems incredible we were able to learn anything in this noisy, uncomfortable place. Students would carry their books back and forth to school each day. Sometimes we had homework to do.

Teachers in the little one-room grade school varied in teaching abilities, from very good to terrible. Everyone in my family was right-handed, except me. When I went to first grade, my teacher was determined that I would use my right hand. When she saw me using my left hand, she would slap my hand with a ruler. That about killed my desire to go to school. There were thirty-five to forty students, so she was very busy. I watched her closely, and when she was not looking, I used my left hand. One day I was using my left hand and didn't notice she was behind me. She grabbed my hair and slammed me up and down in my seat. It hurt very badly. After several weeks of being physically and verbally abused by the teacher, my four older brothers and sisters reported the problem to my parents. Mom and Dad immediately took me took me out of school for the remainder of the year. My dad was on the school board, so this problem was certainly a concern for him. The following year we had a new teacher. I started school again, so Reva and I were in the same grade. The new teacher showed me how to write and allowed me to use my left hand. We got along just fine. He also noticed that my eyes watered when I read small print. Trying to focus strained my eyes. He allowed me to get up and look out the window until my eyes felt better. This understanding and kindhearted teacher was a huge blessing in my life. Without his patience, I would never have been successful in school.

Although he was strict, my second grade teacher, Mr. Cassie Thomas, was also a very good teacher. Thankfully, he was also my teacher in the eighth grade. Mr. Thomas was greatly respected by students. He taught in Canada at one time and often told interesting stories about living there. He was a wonderful teacher who influenced my thoughts about going to high school. Many years later, I rode with him to Columbia, Missouri when I was in college. I was able to tell him how he had been a positive influence in my life.

My third grade teacher was Mr. Austin Griffin, another excellent teacher. In fourth grade, my teacher was Miss Nina Dikes. This year I learned what it was like to have a crush on a teacher. She was a beautiful and kindhearted lady. My fifth and sixth grade teacher was Miss Erma Greenwood. She was loved by all of the students and was an excellent teacher. She had a talent for making us want to learn and to set our goals higher each week. Miss Greenwood did something very unusual in the 1920s. She ran a hot lunch program for the school. She had large kettles of stews and soups simmering on the wood stove for our lunches. She genuinely cared about us. It was easy to work hard for such a caring teacher. I do not know how she accomplished all she did each day. She never slacked in spite of her meager salary.

Our seventh grade teacher was confused and aloof. She did not know what to do, so she just sat in the school yard most of the time. By the end of the year, she did not get out of her buggy all day. Needless to say, we learned nothing that year. We were glad when Mr. Cassie Thomas came back to teach us the next year. Of all our teachers, Reva and I loved Miss Erma Greenwood far more than the others. Miss Greenwood was the aunt of my cousin, Lester Hagan. When she taught at Hickory Grove School, she lived with Uncle Ernest and Aunt Grace, on "the weaning farm." Miss Greenwood was a wonderful piano player, and would entertain friends and family on special occasions. She drove a horse-drawn buggy to school each day.

In the middle of the school day we would stop for lunch. We packed our lunches in a container or pail. We usually had leftovers from supper or breakfast. Sometimes we had peanut butter and jelly sandwiches. A few times I took a large hard-boiled goose egg just to show off. I got a lot of attention for that. Unfortunately it did not taste very good, so I had difficulty swallowing it.

After lunch we had recess time. The girls would play games like drop the handkerchief, or made Jacob's ladders out of yarn. The boys would wrestle and have contests that tested their athletic abilities. Once in a while we would have what we called a pulling match. All we needed was a piece of rope and two teams. We would tie a handkerchief in the middle of the rope and draw two lines in the dirt. The team that could pull the handkerchief past the line on their side was the winning team. In the winter we would play "duck duck goose" in the snow. This involved making a large circle marked into wedges like a pie in the snow. The ducks and the goose played tag but had to stay on the lines. Whatever games we played, we did not have much adult supervision. We made up our own games and rules.

I discovered during those grade school years that I could out-wrestle or out-fight almost any other boy during our roughhousing at recess times. This was probably due to the fact I had bigger brothers who practiced on me. I was also one year older than others in my grade, because I had dropped out of first grade. One time four boys came up to me and said they were going to gang up on me and beat me up. I told them to go ahead, but as fast I could, I would catch each of them by themselves and return the favor, one at a time. They never bothered me after that. The other students respected me and I became a leader by the end of grade school, both in school and during play.

After school, or any time we passed through Mom's kitchen, our eyes would be drawn to a huge rectangular metal box. It was always in sight, and best of all, it was always full of big, thick, soft cookies with sugar sprinkled on top. Mom's cookies were the best in the world. They were light as air and tasted wonderful. The children were allowed to get a cookie any time they were hungry, especially when we arrived home from school. When Mom baked those cookies, the aroma would fill our house and the yard outside.

Erma Greenwood, teacher and the fourth grade class at Hickory Grove School: Left to right, Ray Hagan, Lester Hagan, Leland Larason, Durward Hagan, Reva Hagan

A class picture from Hickory Grove School. Teacher Erma Greenwood is on the back row, right side. Ray Hagan is on row three, left side

SOUVENIR
EDUCATION IS WEALTH

We feel both glad and sad to-day
And scarce can hide the rising tear
We're glad for changes on lifes way
Yet sad to part from schoolmates

HICKORY GROVE SCHOOL
District No. 11
Lindley Twp., Mercer Co., Mo.

ERMA GREENWOOD, Teacher

PUPILS

Francis Spargur	Mildred Hallcroft
Lester Hagan	Raymond Hagan
Reva Hagan	Joe Spargur
Durward Hagan	Leland Larason
Wilma Hagan	Dewey Hagan
Edwin Hagan	Wilford Finney
Doyle Ogle	Darrel Hagan
Irene Spargur	James Spargur
Evelyn Dunn	Lorraine Ogle

Mrs. Allie S. Wilson, Co. Supt.

SCHOOL BOARD

W. L. Hallcroft, Clerk
G. F. Larason, President and Director
Directors
George Hagan   Earnest Hagan

Pearle Hagan's Famous Sugar Cookies

5 cups flour
2 cups sugar
1 teaspoon baking powder
1 teaspoon cream of tartar
½ teaspoon baking soda
2 cups butter, softened
4 eggs
¼ cup milk
1 teaspoon vanilla

Sift together flour, baking powder, cream of tartar, and baking soda. Beat eggs, and then add softened butter, sugar, milk, and vanilla. Mix well, and then add flour a little at a time. Knead until about right to cut into cookies. Before putting in the oven, sprinkle sugar on top of each one. Mom used a very large salt shaker to put sugar on top. Bake 375 for 10 minutes

Chapter 5
CELEBRATING CHRISTMAS COUNTRY STYLE

I have always loved autumn. It was great fun to harvest nuts and apples, then prepare for the upcoming holidays. Every fall we received the Sears Roebuck catalog in the mail. We all loved to look at it, because it contained nearly everything you might want to buy. The girls loved to look at the latest fashions, planning ways they could make their dresses more stylish. There were little order forms in the back. You could fill out the form, and mail it with your money to the Sears Roebuck and Company. A few weeks later you would receive your long-awaited item in the mail. Although I never knew anyone who tried it, you could order kits with everything needed to build a house. The thick catalog had pictures and glowing descriptions of clothing, shoes, candy, hats, and so much more. One time I ordered a leather wallet to carry my money. After it arrived, I realized I had spent all my money on the wonderful wallet and had nothing to put into it. I sent it back, deciding I would rather have the money. When I was a little older, I decided to order my dad something special for Christmas. He loved peanut brittle. I found a very nice box of brittle in the catalog and ordered it for him. It soon came in the mail and I promptly hid it under my bed. I kept looking at it and finally decided I ought to taste it to see if it was good. It was. I had one more piece. It was good too. Pretty soon the entire box was empty. I had to order another one. By the time Christmas came, the second box was about half-empty. Dad never said anything about it, except, "Thank you for the wonderful present."

In preparation for the Christmas season, Mom and Dad would take us to town so we could do a little shopping. Raycel and I used the money we earned selling fur pelts, to buy little items for each of our family members and special friends. On Christmas Eve, we hung up our stockings. Even my parents would hang a stocking. We would place the presents we had for one another next to their stocking. We all enjoyed singing Christmas carols while Jessie, Vee or Reva played the piano in the parlor. This was the only time we were allowed in the parlor.

One Christmas Eve after hanging our stockings, Mom and Dad sent us to bed. We were all very excited, talking, laughing, playing and looking out the window. We could not seem to settle down. All at once we heard sleigh bells! Mom told us Santa would not come unless we were in bed with our heads covered up! We all ran for our beds and strained to hear the bells again. Later I realized this was our neighbors going down the road in their horse-drawn sleigh. They used the sleigh when the roads were covered with snow and ice.

On Christmas morning our stockings would be full. We were not allowed to look inside them until we had eaten breakfast. I was never very hungry. We were excited as we pulled out peppermint candy, socks, hankies, and small toys. One time Raycel and I each got a pocketknife. That was a wonderful surprise.

Mother always fixed a big dinner on Christmas Day, complete with desserts. The Christmas menu depended on what foods had done well on the farm that year. We often had a large ham or a goose. One dessert that appeared every Christmas was a wonderful fruitcake. I did not like other fruitcakes when I grew up, because they did not taste like Mom's fruitcake, which actually was more like candy.

Bethel Church, our wonderful family church, had a big Christmas celebration every year. The ladies cooked a special Christmas Eve lunch. They served several kinds of meat, dressing, apple salad, fresh rolls and many desserts. We always had a huge decorated Christmas tree. The smell of evergreen filled the church, along with the aroma of hot bread. Under the tree were many presents. We all gave gifts to our friends, cousins, aunts and uncles. The gifts were little items such as hair ribbons or barrettes. The adults gave each other gifts as well. One year the tree was decorated with dolls for all the little girls. Everyone received a gift. Some gifts would be wrapped with little tags on them. The ladies might get an embroidered tea towel carefully rolled up and tied with a little ribbon, or a small kitchen item.

One year a gigantic lady's corset was carefully wrapped in pretty paper and given to one of the men. This was met with great shouts of laughter. He was quite surprised and embarrassed. For many years following, that same corset made an appearance, going from one person to another, causing outbursts of laughter.

Trays of mouthwatering homemade candies were passed around. Santa would arrive each year and bring a bag of candy for everyone. One year Mrs.

Claus came, dressed up in white and red. Mrs. Claus was my Aunt Bessie, Jim Hagan's wife.

On the evening of the Christmas program, the church filled with people. Every year we had a live nativity scene and someone would read the Christmas story. When I was little, Aunt Gertrude Shirley enjoyed helping and would play piano for quartets and soloists taking part in the program. Because he had a wonderful voice, Albert always sang, either a solo, or with a quartet. My mother and other women would also help with the program, playing piano or making sure that everyone was in their places and ready to go to the front of the church to take their turn. Almost everyone took part in some way, from the very young to the elderly, even making sure the entire church was decorated. Uncle Willy Shirley always gave a big talk and the children would sing songs and recite poems. Mom would have her Sunday school class sing together and say scripture verses. I gave a talk when I was nine years old, and recited a poem about a church. During my speech I told a story about a raccoon that came up and looked in the church window. I became very excited about my story and yelled out, "Woooo! Woooo!" The adults laughed until they cried. I finally decided that meant they liked it. At the end of the program we all joined together to sing Christmas Carols. Several years later, cousin Veta Hagan and Agnes Eastin were in charge of the Christmas programs, Veta would send away for plays and put them on at Christmas time.

Pearle Hagan's Uncooked Christmas Fruitcake

1lb dates
1lb marshmallows
1lb candy orange slices
½ cup sugar
1lb graham crackers
1 cup chopped nuts
1 cup whipped cream
raisins

Cut the dates, orange slices and marshmallows in small pieces and mix together. Add sugar, whipped cream and chopped nuts. Roll graham crackers into fine crumbs. Add to mixture and work with hands until all is moist and mixed well. Press into a loaf pan lined with waxed paper or aluminum foil. Let stand a week or 10 days in the ice box. Keep tightly wrapped to prevent it from drying out. Slice and serve.

Chapter 6
LIVING THE COUNTRY LIFE

*S*hortly after Darrell was born, I was at the barn watching my two older brothers, Albert and Raycel, feed the livestock. My father had warned me to stay away from an old ram that was getting mean. I was walking around the barn on my way to the house when the ram saw me. He took after me, and head-butted me, knocking me to the ground. He would let me get up and run about twenty feet away, then knock me down again. I screamed as loudly as I could. That old ram outweighed me by about two hundred pounds. I made it around the barn about the time my older brothers came to my rescue. Dad made sure that ram was next in line for market.

We had a nice house and made several improvements over the years. However, it was small for a family of nine by today's standards. The parlor was located on the front of the house. One parlor window had a table in front of it with a kerosene lamp in the middle. If there was an urgent matter and Mom needed Dad during the day, she would light this lamp as a signal for him to come home. She did this on the day I was born. My brothers and sisters and I could not go into the parlor. It was absolutely off limits to children. It looked very nice with wallpaper, fancy oil lamps, and an unusual, round, wooden rocking chair and a pretty rug. The parlor furniture was the only furniture that never wore out.

My parents slept downstairs in a small bedroom. There was a tiny nursery adjacent to their bedroom. I stayed in the nursery with baby Reva for a while. There were two bedrooms upstairs. Albert and Raycel were in one bedroom and Jesse and Vee were in the other. I was moved in with Raycel when Darrell, my youngest brother, took over the nursery. At times there were three children in each bedroom upstairs.

We had a wood stove for heat in the cold winters. It worked well in the room where it was located, which was the middle of the house downstairs, but the farther away you got from it the colder it was. We would stand near it and warm up one side, then turn around and warm up the other side. The upstairs bedrooms were very cold indeed. I slept with Raycel for many years. He would pull all the covers away from me when he was sleeping. He was older and bigger, but I finally figured out how to wrap the edge of the blanket around one leg and hold on with both hands as best as I could. Mom made our quilts, feather tick mattresses and pillows. She would pile on so many covers we could feel their weight. That helped to alleviate the cold a little bit. We could see our breath in the rooms upstairs, and the windowpanes iced over on cold nights. We all wore long underwear in the winter. In summertime the upstairs was stifling hot. We left windows open in hopes of feeling a little breeze. We tried not to go upstairs until bedtime to avoid the intense heat. We learned to sleep in adverse conditions.

Outside, Dad added two ponds for watering the livestock. He bought fish in Pleasanton, Iowa to stock the ponds. My brothers and I enjoyed going fishing and eating our catch for supper. Throughout my childhood, swimming was my favorite activity in the summer time. I have fond memories about the largest pond that was used as a favorite swimming hole. People came for miles around to swim there and I went swimming with every group that came along. I learned to swim at an early age, about four or five years old. I heard all kinds of stories during those years, many of which I didn't understand. One time I told one of the stories to Mother. She laughed a little, but told me to never tell anybody else. When I was older, I figured out that it was really what we would call a dirty joke.

During summer vacations from school, my brothers and I worked on the farm alongside Dad. All year long, everyone in the family had chores to do. It was vital that we all worked to make the farms and our lives run smoothly. Many animals depended on us for food, water and their upkeep. Every morning of their lives, my parents were up at four o'clock. They would dress, pray together, and then Dad would begin chores while Mom started breakfast. Dad ate his breakfast after milking the cows. The children had assigned chores to be completed before and after school. We would bring in firewood for the cook stove and heating stove, gather eggs, haul in water, and feed the chickens. Sometimes we milked the cows. My sister, Vee and I would tie the cow's tails to the fence so they would not hit us in the face while we were milking them. I am not sure the cows liked this idea quite as well as Vee and I did.

When we got a little older, my brothers and I worked in the fields alongside Dad. Because we raised livestock, hay was a very important commodity on our farm. I admired my dad for the way he could make an extremely large haystack. We had mostly timothy and a little clover hay. Several implements were needed to make those gigantic piles of hay. In late summer we cut hay with a horse-drawn mowing machine. After cutting the hay, we would use a sulkey rake and

My father is on top of the haystack. I am leading the ricker horse.

I am on top of the haystack with my dad, Ross Hagan. A large ricker fork is in the front.

put the hay into rows. With a bull rake and two horses we would take large bunches of hay to the ricker by the haystack. A ricker was a piece of equipment with a gigantic fork similar to a pitchfork. It was used to throw hay on top of a big haystack, and was powered by one horse pulling the ricker. My job was to lead the ricker's horse. When I got older, I ran the sulkey rake to throw hay to one side in rounds. I sat on a little seat, stomped a pedal and it would make a pile. We stored hay in the loft of the big red barn. That made getting hay to the cows easier. From the loft, we sent it down the chutes directly to the cattle.

Cash crops cultivated on our farm included wheat and corn. Other crops such as oats and hay were cultivated for farm use. At a time when few farmers were aware of the necessity, my dad rotated crops for better soil conservation. When the grains matured, we used a horse-drawn binder to harvest it. One of my brothers would stand several of the bundles vertically with a bundle or two on top. This would keep them from getting too wet during the rains. After a month or two, it would be time to thresh the grains. We waited until someone with a huge threshing machine came to our farm. My brothers and I would throw the sheaves on the wagon to take it to the threshing machine, and then throw the tied bundles of wheat or oats into the threshing machine to thresh out the grain. These grains were stored inside the barn. We had an oat crib and a separate corn crib. We used teams of horses to plant and harvest the corn. The corn was planted in rows about three feet apart. When the corn started to grow, we would take a horse-drawn cultivator down the rows to keep the weeds from growing.

Our farm was a business. Dad raised registered Hereford cattle. He never considered another breed. He was convinced this was the best kind of beef cattle available and took great care in breeding, raising and showing them. He was influenced by my grandfather, Robert Hagan, who brought the first purebred Herefords to Mercer County. The cattle became Dad's main emphasis and cash income. He was widely recognized for breeding, raising, and selling Herefords. I remember being with him in the barnyard as he pumped water for them into the stock tank with an old hand pump while the cows milled around on the other side of the fence.

To sell the cattle, we would drive them to the stockyards in Mercer, Missouri. There were large cattle pens located just past the downtown area. On one particular cattle drive, I was riding a horse while Dad, Albert and Raycel were walking with the cattle to keep them moving forward. My job was to ride ahead and block off side roads and driveways to keep the cattle on course. When we entered Mercer, one cow got upset and began to chase people. The crazed animal chased two men around a car until they were able to jump into their vehicle. The animal spotted another man sitting on a porch in front of a local business. He was about four feet off the ground, with his legs dangling off of the edge of the porch. The cow charged with her head down. The man quickly raised his legs

Ross Hagan's First Car & Uncle Jim's Car
Ross Paid - $375
Raymond on fender of 1919 Model T

Raymond with Raycel's Calf

and rolled backwards. The cow head-butted the porch so hard she was stunned. This gave Raycel and Albert an opportunity to get their ropes around her. Dad and I hustled to get the rest of the cattle into the pen. We finally completed our cattle drive and successfully sold all the Herefords to a man headed to the Kansas City Stockyards. That was a long day's work.

Dad kept horses for transportation and farm use. He loved good horses, and always tried to match his teams of horses in size and strength. He was wise about selecting horses with personalities suited to the jobs they were expected to do. He was a natural horseman and was known for his ability to train a horse well. He also raised registered, Spotted Poland China hogs, which we butchered and cured for our own use, pure-bred Hampshire sheep, Jersey cows for milk, and for cream and butter to sell, and Rhode Island Red laying hens to sell their eggs. We also raised turkeys and geese.

Dad designed and built a unique house for his chickens. It had three rooms. Two rooms had horizontal shelves for nests where chickens would lay eggs and one for hatching eggs, the third room was a separate area where they would roost for the night. The room intended for them to roost had a sleeping shelf that was on an incline from the floor up to the ceiling so they could get to the top. In the egg laying room, Dad made a shelf about two feet above the floor with one square foot box for each hen. The nesting room was where they hatched eggs. Dad had feed and water available for them so they could sit on the nests and have everything they needed close by. I checked the nests each evening and put the eggs in a big bucket. This chicken house was toured by many people from our farming community, and a picture appeared in the local newspaper because it had a well thought out design. Dad's chicken house is still standing after over 100 years. This structure is used on the farm today for other purposes.

Ross and Pearle Hagan in front of their innovative chicken house

My parents were always progressive in farming techniques and tried to learn new and better ways to run their business. Dad was an active member of the Missouri Hereford Association. One of the things my parents did was sponsor the West Side Farm Club. This organization provided regular meetings to share ideas and information through speakers and literature about all aspects of farm life.

Chapter 7
"Ohhhh, Mama's cookin!"

My mother was an excellent cook. She never sat down at the table when the family ate. She was always running from kitchen to dining room, trying to serve everyone. She cooked delicious meals with a great variety of vegetables, bread and desserts. Our dinner table always had an assortment of jams, jellies and honey. Like all farm wives in this era, Mom home canned all our vegetables, fruits, and even meat in glass jars.

We had a special building for smoking meat. This is how we preserved it, so it would not spoil. We ate a lot of pork. Dad butchered several hogs each year, and then smoked the meat. We had ham, bacon, sausage, and sliced cured pork. Smoking hams and bacon is a slow process. Many farms had a smokehouse large enough for the meat of several hogs to be cured, and then hung from the rafters to be smoked and aged. Often the roof was steeply pitched to provide additional hanging space. The eaves were vented to allow air movement and avoid stale smoke. This curing and aging process eliminated the risk of trichinosis. I loved the wonderful smell of smoking meats that lingered in the smokehouse even when it was empty.

In the spring we had fresh chickens. My mother's chicken and dumplings were wonderful. Her dumplings were very tiny; just about an inch long and light and fluffy. Gravy was a mainstay, served with nearly all meats. Mom made the gravy in the same cast iron pans she cooked the meat. Pan drippings make the very best gravy. A special crock was positioned near the cook stove to hold the drippings from fried bacon. It was saved to be used as seasoning for vegetables like green beans. It was also used in place of oil when frying potatoes or eggs. Nothing was wasted. When Mom would fry chicken, she put the wishbone on a dish in the cupboard. After everyone had eaten their dinner, she would enjoy her favorite piece of chicken. Vee's favorite piece of the chicken was the feet.

Mom always made sure everyone in her home had a full tummy before she took a bite. She was totally selfless in all of her actions. In the mornings, Mom would drink coffee with lots of cream. Many times I saw her pour coffee into the saucer under her cup to allow it to cool down before she drank it. My dad would drink hot water rather than coffee. He would add sugar and sometimes cream to his hot water.

Our breakfasts were big and filling. We had eggs, with bacon, sausage or ham, and sometimes biscuits, or cornmeal mush fried in bacon drippings until it was crispy. Oatmeal was served occasionally, as was cereal with milk or cream fresh from our Jersey cows. All of these wonderful meals were cooked on a wood-burning cooking stove. Leftovers were placed in the middle of the table, covered with a snow white tea towel, and saved for lunches and snacks. Mother's kitchen was meticulously clean. The floors were swept after all meals and hand scrubbed each day. Counters, tabletops and even the windowsills were constantly washed. Any scraps and fruit and vegetable peelings would go into a bucket for the hogs. The bucket was kept out of sight behind the cooking stove and emptied after supper. This was a supplement to their diet. Nothing was wasted. We reused and recycled everything before this was fashionable. We just thought we were being wise, rather than wasteful.

Our meals were based on what we were able to produce on the farm. My mother cooked what was in season, or what she had carefully preserved. We had one of the largest and most diversified fruit orchards in North Missouri. My parents planted various cultivars of apples, peaches, cherries, plums, as well as various nuts. Rows of grape vines produced bumper crops, located near the fenced gardens. One day Dad was working in the fields when a man stopped by and asked if he could look at our orchard. Of course Dad was agreeable. The man said he was traveling the countryside trying to find cultivars of good fruit trees to use as root stock. The man and his brothers were trying to develop a line of better fruit trees. They had a long conversation and Dad allowed him to take any cuttings he desired. The man's last name was Stark. In later years, Stark Brothers Nurseries became well known fruit tree wholesalers. They advertised a better rootstock and claimed greater fruit production from their fine trees.

Like both of my grandfathers, Dad was a beekeeper. Honeybees require care and maintenance. Dad bought fifteen hives and placed them at the edge of the pasture behind the chicken house. Keeping honeybees near crops ensures a greater harvest. Each hive will ultimately produce over fifty pounds of honey per year. We had honey to sell and enough to share with others. Honey was always on our dining table. When harvesting honey, Dad would wear a large hood with a face cover, and a special jacket with long sleeves to prevent bee stings. He also had a little hand-held smoker. He would light the smoker using dry leaves and twigs. The smoke seemed to slow the bee's reaction time, making them eat honey and become pacified. Honey was served in the honeycomb with our meals, ready to put on hot bread, toast, biscuits and pancakes. I still eat honey every day.

Our garden was huge. We grew green beans, cabbage, tomatoes, potatoes, sweet potatoes, rhubarb, onions, peas, cucumbers, spinach, turnip greens, collard greens, and lettuce. One of my favorites was a very large golden yellow squash called cashaws. Mom made it into pies similar to a pumpkin pie. I loved those pies. One afternoon after school, Raycel and I walked into the kitchen and saw five of those freshly baked pies sitting out to cool for our supper. Raycel got one of the pies and a fork and sat down and proceeded to eat the whole pie. My mouth watered while I wondered if he would get into trouble. I finally gave in and got my own fork and pie to enjoy. Mom never mentioned the missing pies. My parents took vegetables and honey to Pleasanton, Iowa and Saline, Missouri to sell. I remember Mom selling a dozen eggs for fifty cents, which was about the same price as a pound of coffee. My parents tried growing many different things. If they heard about it, they would try to grow it, and then it would appear on our dinner table.

In the corner of the corn field, we grew pumpkins, watermelons and cantaloupes. Sometimes on a hot summer afternoon, Raycel and I would go there and take a watermelon into the shady cornfield and eat it. I learned from Raycel how to thump a melon to see if it was ripe, and to be sure it had a yellow spot on the bottom. Dad grew such a variety of things that people would come just to see it all.

Dad built a large two-room underground "cave" close behind the house to store and preserve garden produce and Mom's home canned foods. The "cave," or root cellar, remained cool enough to keep our fruit, including apples and melons, edible almost year around. I can remember eating apples in the springtime that had been kept in the cave all winter. We would carefully sort them often to be sure there were no rotten apples. This cave also served as a storm shelter during tornado season. The wooden steps leading to the cave were located behind a wooden door.

Mom became known for her cooking and won numerous awards for her canned foods at the county fair. One year she won a blue ribbon for her canned peaches. She set up that jar where we could all admire it. In spite of our giggles, she took it to the fair the following year and again won a blue ribbon. Her pickled peaches were delicious. I believe anything made with fresh peaches is good. Mom and my sisters made peach butter and sealed it in jars. Peach butter is similar to apple butter. It is excellent on hot biscuits. They made many kinds of jams, jellies and butters from our fruit crops. We had mulberry trees, but their fruits were not well-respected. Mom would lay sheets on the ground and have the children shake the trees to harvest the mulberries. She made them into jelly, sometimes mixing them with grapes. Canning fruits required a great deal of sugar. I recall Mom paying thirty-five cents for five pounds of sugar at the grocery store in Saline, in the mid-1920s.

Mom cooked for the threshers during harvest. She and the other women would prepare huge quantities of fried chicken, ham, mashed potatoes and gravy, breads, vegetables, and white corn. Mom made pumpkin, cherry, apple, and walnut pies. She would have tables on the front and back porches loaded with food for the men to eat. The tables were covered with nice tablecloths. Drinks were served in glass fruit jars. At each place at the table were individual salt cellars. This is a small round dish used to hold salt. Food could be dipped into the salt as desired. The women seemed to work harder than the men in the fields. After feeding them, Mom and my sisters would wash massive piles of dishes and tablecloths and then begin cooking desserts for the next day.

Mom made the best light bread I ever tasted. Once a week she would make enough loaves to feed our family of nine. Jesse, Vee and Reva helped her. She frequently made biscuits, cutting them with a round tin cutter. She also made butter from our Jersey cows' milk. We kept just enough Jerseys cows to provide our milk and butter and a little extra to sell. Mom had a couple types of churns. One of them was a square glass container with several wooden paddles inside. The large metal top screwed on and had a handle that we turned around and around until we saw the butter form. Even the smallest children in our family helped turn the handle.

Mom did not use a written recipe for bread or biscuits. She would add fistfuls of flour and knead it until it "looked right." When she made cakes or other baked goods, she would add a specific number of eggshells of milk or water, rather than using measuring cups. We had dessert almost every day. She made cakes, cookies, and pumpkin and rhubarb pies. I have always been fond of chocolate. Mom made a chocolate dessert that I can still see and taste in my mind. It was a cross between pudding and cake, warm, moist and rich.

Pearle's Chocolate Upside-down Cake

In a bowl, beat the following batter well. Spread evenly in the bottom of a square cake pan.

1 cup flour
¾ cup sugar
2 tablespoons cocoa
2 teaspoons baking powder
sift these dry ingredients together a few times.
Add ½ cup milk
1 teaspoon vanilla
2 tablespoons Butter

Set aside as you prepare this to pour over the top;
4 tablespoons of cocoa
¾ cup brown sugar
1 ½ cups boiling water

Pour this on the top and bake at 400 degrees for 35 to 40 minutes.

Mom served this with a spoonful of fresh whipped cream on top. Delicious while still warm from the oven.

Chapter 8

GROWING UP HAGAN

 Every Hagan I have ever known had a solid hard work ethic. No job was too small or beneath us. Children observed and learned we were to do a job well and to completion. We were raised with the understanding that life was as good as we were willing to make it. If we desired to have money in our pockets, we needed to earn it. Every winter, Raycel and I had a little business venture to earn money. We would trap skunks, civet cats, opossum, and raccoons. On the way to school in the mornings, we checked our traps. Several times when we were in grade school, Raycel and I got sprayed by the skunks and civet cats. One day the teacher sent me home from school because I had been sprayed and smelled very badly. Mom washed us down and soaked our clothes to get rid of the strong odor. Tomato juice helped the smell go away. The traps we used were spring type traps. We set them with bait that we purchased. Raycel and I sold rabbits for meat as well as the pelts.

 We would skin the animals and stretch the skins on a board until they dried out. This was time-consuming and often more than a little messy. We considered it well worth the effort when we sold the pelts at a fur business in Pleasanton, Iowa. That was the way we made a little money. Skunk skin was worth more than the other skins. We were able to get one dollar for a skunk skin and less for civet cat, rabbit and opossum pelts. Raycel and I might have been the only ones willing to trap those malodorous creatures, making skunk skins more valuable! The furrier sold our animal skins to be made into ladies' fine coat collars and hats.

 One day I saw an advertisement in a newspaper giving a glowing report of how I could make great amounts of money selling Cloverine Salve. I ordered my kit by mail and began selling it by going door to door. I did pretty well for a while. One day I went to a house and made my best pitch to the lady answering the door. She asked, "How much?" When I told her she said, "Just a minute." I soon heard a little girl crying, "No, Mommy, NO! Please don't take my money!" My heart ached for a little girl I had never seen. That ended my efforts as a salesman forever. To this day I have no desire to be in sales.

Dad truly enjoyed animals of all kinds. He taught his children to treat animals with respect and kindness. He had a special affinity for collie dogs. They seemed to match Dad's kind and gentle personality. The collies were loyal and quick to learn. They would defend any of us if we needed it, but were very sweet animals most of the time. One time a man brought his collie to our house. He talked Dad into letting the two dogs fight. The most unusual thing happened. Dad's collie stood up on his hind legs and began moving his front paws left and right, almost like a man. It was upsetting to the other dog. Those dogs fought viciously for a bit, but then Dad stopped it. I was glad! I felt sure they would have fought until one of them was killed.

A pack of wild dogs roamed the countryside near our farm. They were hunting as a team, taking down various farm animals. One of our collies ran away and joined them. The area farmers were trying to get rid of the wild dogs. The neighbors told us they had seen our collie running in the pack. We knew we would never see him again. One morning we found him lying on the porch near the back door. Dad said to be very careful, as we could no longer trust him. He slipped around the house and shut the porch door. We gave the dog food and water and did not let him run freely for many days. We were finally able to calm him down and tame him again. It was unusual to tame a dog that had been wild. My father had a great understanding of animal behavior and how to train them.

Mom taught each one of her children to take care of their brothers and sisters. The older children were responsible to protect and watch the younger children. One day, my younger brother, Darrell and I were playing in the garden, located in our back yard. I was in fourth grade, nearly eleven years old, and Darrell was five years old. The garden was surrounded by a tall, woven wire fence with barbed wire on the top to keep out the animals. Otherwise rabbits, chickens and dogs would have done great damage to our vegetables. We were in the back part of the garden and decided to go into the orchard. The quickest way to get to the orchard was to climb over the fence. I climbed up next to a post and went up the woven wire fencing by placing my feet between the wires. I made it over the barbed wire and down to the other side. Little Darrell followed my example and climbed up to the top, but was afraid to go over the barbed wire. The collie dog waited patiently for us in the orchard. I climbed back up to get Darrell. I leaned over the fence with one hand on the fence post and one on the wire. I told Darrell to climb up and get on my back. He climbed up the fence and onto my back and hung on tightly to my neck. I had one arm over the barbed wire to hold it down and my other hand gripping the post. I thought I could just let loose and jump down with Darrell on my back. When I let loose, my arm caught on the sharp barbs. The wicked barbs caught my arm halfway between my elbow and wrist, ripping my arm open all the way to my wrist. It was appallingly, terribly painful, but I was careful not to let Darrell know how badly I was injured.

I took the side road, which was easier than getting back over the fence, but we still had to go under another barbed wire fence. Thankfully, this one was open near the ground. Darrell saw my arm bleeding and realized it was ripped open. He started screaming I put my left hand over the gaping wound and we crawled under the barbed wire fence and made it to the road. This road intersected with the main road that ran in front of our home. Darrell was crying and ran ahead of me. Rather than turning left toward the house, he panicked and began running the other way, heading straight to the Little River. Vee and the collie dog heard us and came to our rescue. Vee was barefooted, but ran as quickly as she could and caught Darrell, while I slowly made my way back to the house. The collie stayed close by my side. Mother immediately elevated my arm and determined this was a very serious injury. She tried to clean me up a little and put a clean white tea towel over my arm.

My father and older brothers were putting up hay near Uncle Arthur Finney's place. Mom called the Finney's home and said to get word to Dad I was badly hurt. Dad rushed home on horseback. He put me in the car and drove as quickly as possible to the doctor's office in Cainsville. I had complete trust in my dad to care for me. When we got there, the doctor looked me over carefully. He said that not only had barbs cut the flesh on my arm, but it had cut two or three ligaments, as well as the largest muscle.

The doctor strapped both of my arms to a chair. It was a big chair resembling a barber's chair that shifted up and down. The doctor told Dad to get behind me and hold my head, placing one of his hands on my chin and mouth and the other hand on my forehead. The old country doctor put stitches in the ligaments that were almost torn in two. He pulled the muscles together and sewed them so they would stay. He finally stitched the skin together so it would cover the gaping wound. He did not give me anything to dull the pain. It was impossible to move or cry out because of the way my Dad held my head. I just sat and watched, in spite of the pain. Finally he said, "I think that will be all right." He put a large quantity of white powder on the wound and covered my arm with a white cloth bandage before we left. In that time, it was believed physical pain will pass if it is ignored. I assure you, I felt great pain. My injuries healed after nearly two months. The strength in that arm was diminished for several months longer. I still have jagged scars on my arm.

My mom was introduced to a woman in our community who gave piano lessons in her students' homes. After living through a few catastrophes that occurred raising seven active children, Mom thought a few piano lessons might tame us a bit. Playing piano was great fun. I looked forward to my lesson each week. When harvest time came, I had to quit taking lessons so I could help with cutting grain. The piano teacher kept asking Mom where I was and when I would continue lessons. She told my mom I had talent and suggested she should not allow me to quit taking lessons. It was my choice. I wanted to continue with piano lessons, but felt I had to help my dad with the harvest. Jessie, Vee and Reva could read music and played the piano very well. Music and playing the piano were very enjoyable to me. In the evenings, I made up my own songs on the piano.

Being a Hagan meant you were a member of a very large clan. I had fun with the numerous Hagan cousins in my family. Many of them were in school with me and some went to Bethel Church as well. We were close, and many of us stayed in contact all of our lives. When we were young, the Hagan family frequently had big family "get-togethers" with aunts, uncles, and cousins of all ages. I always enjoyed playing with my cousin, Hubert Hagan, one of Jim Hagan's sons. I especially liked Hubert because he was friendly and kind-hearted. He was older than me and I respected him as being wise. We were always ready to try something new and exciting.

At one of these family "get-togethers" at Jim Hagan's farm north of Freedom Church, several of the younger cousins were playing outside near the pond. Hubert (about age ten), Lloyd, and I (about age seven) were there. Hubert had an idea that sounded interesting. On the hill near the pond was a round or cylindrical metal water tank about five feet in diameter. Hubert thought one of us, specifically me, should hunker down inside the tank, and then the other boys could roll it down the hill, into the pond. After a great deal of discussion, Hubert talked me into trying this out. He was pretty persuasive. I climbed inside the tank in a crouched and uncomfortable position. The other boys started running and rolling the tank down the hillside. With every roll my body weight would shift from my feet to the top of my head inside the hard metal tank. They were all laughing and shouting when the tank, with me inside, hit the water. Fortunately, the tank finally righted itself and I was able to climb out. It was a wild and bumpy ride. After rubbing my sore head for a while, I helped the other boys take a turn. It was an exciting day for us all. Hubert was pretty creative and full of fun. After we grew up, Hubert remained the same: friendly, kind, and deserving my respect.

Chapter 9

THE INFLUENCE THAT GUIDED ME

Sunday school and church were a must for our family. Every Sunday we would pile into a wagon or car and head to Bethel Church. When I got a little older, I liked to ride a horse to church. My mother taught Sunday school for many years, and my dad was on the board. Church was an important part of our lives. It was there I learned about the Bible, the existence of the Lord Jesus Christ and an after-life consisting of heaven and hell. To a young boy, heaven and hell seemed almost like a fairy tale. I was more interested in riding horses, pitching a baseball and hunting than thinking about life after death. My grandmother, Sarah Hagan had passed away, but she seemed very old to me. It would be many years before I had to worry about dying. I enjoyed the many Bible stories that were taught every week, especially the one about David and Goliath. He was small like me, but challenged a giant. David was an overcomer.

    I enjoyed singing hymns with the piano for accompaniment, just like my mother. Her favorite song was "Bringing in the Sheaves." Many years later, this song was sung at her funeral at Bethel Church. I thought my heart would break. I learned how to live in a Christ-like manner by observing my parents' lives. They never argued, or said a cross word to each other. They demonstrated a life of love, respect for each other, and for those around them. I never heard my parents say an unkind word about anyone. They prayed out loud before meals and during other times of prayer. I did not realize how unusual this was, until I grew up and observed how others live. I was blessed by God with good parents. They were a beacon of integrity, compassion and strength.

    I recall attending revivals at Bethel when the church would fill up with people. One specific revival in June of 1926 changed my life. I was eleven years old when two women evangelists came for revival. The main evangelist was Miss Violet. It was a huge event. Our family went every night for two weeks. The evangelists stayed in our home for several days, as well as in the homes of other Bethel members. Because they spoke plainly, their words made sense to me. I began to understand that at conception our bodies start to grow around our spirit. Our spirit is placed into that tiny body by God. I had never considered that my body was not all of me, and I would live on after my body died.

> Eccl 12:7
> "And the dust returns to the earth as it was, and the spirit returns to God who gave it."

Many people, including my sister Jessie, other siblings and cousins, went to the altar to dedicate their lives to the Lord Jesus. The messages we heard explained how to be sure we would go to heaven when we died. Miss Violet, the main evangelist, stated that those who did not go to heaven would end up in hell. This was a very frightening thought to me. She made the spiritual realm seem real. I learned that believers in Jesus Christ became citizens of heaven, according to the Bible.

> Philippians 3:20-21
> "But our citizenship is in heaven. And we eagerly await a Savior from there, the Lord Jesus Christ, who, by the power that enables him to bring everything under his control, will transform our lowly bodies so that they will be like his glorious body." (NIV)

Miss Violet had a daughter about twelve years old. She was the prettiest little girl I had ever seen. During the service one night, she came to me and said, "Why don't you go to the altar and be saved." I said I had been thinking about it. She said, "Come on and I will go with you." We knelt at the altar together, along with many others. I prayed for the Lord to make me part of His kingdom and forgive me of my sins, like the evangelist said to do. I heard the little girl pray, "Dear Lord, forgive him of his sins and guide him in everything he says and does." I have used those words in my prayers every day, all of my life. Several days later, over twenty people, many of them my relatives, and Jessie and I, went to Little River and were baptized. This was a public testimony of the change in our lives. Our sins were washed away and we became followers of Jesus. We followed the example of Jesus when John baptized him. Some decisions we make as children affect our lives forever. The commitment I made

The influence that guided me

to Christ as a young boy has been a lifelong covenant for me. I made this decision when I knelt at the altar in Bethel Church.

In the following weeks I began to realize that death is not the end, but the beginning. If we have given our hearts and lives to Jesus, the Bible says to be absent from our bodies is to be present with the Lord. I finally understood that my grandmother, Sarah Hagan was repositioned into my future, awaiting my arrival in heaven. I understood that it is fine to bury our bodies in a cemetery, but the important part of us, our spirit, lives on forever.

Chapter 10

FAMILY TIES

A ridiculous accident taught me how important it is to ask the Lord for direction every day. I am pretty sure it would have altered the decision I was about to make. Using my limited knowledge of physics, I developed a plan to move a very large rock in the schoolyard. I used a 14' x 2" x 12" board, left over from a bridge construction, and another rock as a lever. We tied a rope around the board and rock. We tied jump ropes to the end of the board to help in the process of moving it. Many of the students pulled down on the rope to move the rock. The rope kept slipping off the bottom of the rock. I bent over to see if it was tied securely when the kids began to pull down again. The board snapped off and hit me squarely in the face. The tremendous force completely flipped my body over and knocked me out. My nose was literally flattened on my face. My nose was not just broken, but was completely smashed.

When I regained consciousness, the teacher had my head in her lap, trying to stop the bleeding. She sent me to the Larasons' farm near the school. The doctor was busy and could not come, so Mrs. Larason stuffed my nose full of cotton before my parents picked me up. Without medical care, my nose never healed properly. Breathing became very difficult and affected every day of my life. This unfortunate accident is an example of the way our community of friends and family stuck together; always ready to help others in time of need.

When we needed groceries or supplies, we would go "trading" at the local grocery store. We would sell what we raised, or made, to the store owner. That provided money to buy what we needed; staples such as flour, sugar, coffee and other supplies as well. One day Mom and I were waiting in line with fresh eggs to trade and to buy groceries. The woman in line ahead of us brought in butter to trade. She gave her grocery list to the store owner, who took it to the back and proceeded to fill the order she wanted as trade for the butter.

The store owner came out from the back and said, "Ma'am, you just brought butter to sell, but you have butter on your list."

"I know," whispered the lady, "but rats got into it. I thought what they don't know won't hurt them."

The store keeper filled her grocery order and the woman left. Mom said that she needed a pound of butter, but didn't think she wanted any at this time. The clerk said, "Oh, don't you worry honey, it's okay, she took the same butter home with her. I just went back and put it in another container." She smiled at Mom and said, "What she doesn't know won't hurt her!"

We did laundry once a week. Laundry day was a huge effort and required the labor of several family members to accomplish the job in a timely manner. Vee and I were now old enough to be assigned this task. Sometimes we made lye soap to be used for laundry and baths. Mom would occasionally buy soap powder and borax at the general store. I used to run the washing machine by myself. It consisted of a large round metal tub with a wooden handle running through it. We would heat water on the cook-stove in the kitchen, and carry the hot water out to the washing machine on the back porch. I would put in the water, add the soap and then add the clothes. I would run it by pulling the wooden handle back and forth. The handle made the clothes "agitate" in the tub. The next tub had rinse water. Vee would use a wringer to squeeze the water out of the laundry. It looked like two rolling pins mounted very close together, spinning in circles. She had a couple of incidents with that wringer. One time she got her long hair caught in it. She was nearly scalped before Mom could save her. Another time she got her hand caught in it and mashed her fingers and hand. It was very painful when her little, thin arm was pulled into the wringer almost to her elbow. After washing, rinsing twice, and wringing, we would hang the laundry on an outdoor clothesline. Diapers were washed in a separate load. The sunshine would help whiten the clothes, or a few drops of liquid bluing could be added to the water. Next Jessie, Reva, and Vee would iron the clothes and pillowcases with heavy "sad irons" that were heated on the wood stove. Needless to say, this was a full day's work.

When I was in fourth grade, we moved to Granddad Hagan's place. He was getting older and my grandmother had passed away. Granddad needed someone to help him work the farm and take care of him and his house as well. He was very persuasive when asking my parents to move to his home. I remember him telling the reasons they needed to move in with him. He and Dad had farmed together for many years and worked well together. Often I heard him say he "loved Pearle's cooking" and the way she kept her home sparkling clean. Granddad was very friendly and always had a smile on his face. He was also aggressive and extremely persuasive. My dad was different from his father in this way. Dad was an unassuming, quiet man who knew what needed to be done and did it without comment. He had opinions, of course, but I never heard him attempt to persuade others to follow his desires.

We were a close-knit family and would help each other in time of need. I knew my grandfather missed his wife of over fifty years. It would have been uncomfortable to move Granddad to our small house, as there was no bedroom for him. His house was bigger, so we moved our belongings, our horses, chickens, collies and everything we needed to live, down the road to Granddad's house. We shut our house up and would check on it now and then. My father, with assistance from his sons, continued to work on both farms as he had for many years. That was a lot of acreage and we all worked hard the years we lived there. Granddad kept half of the income from the farm. Dad earned shares, or a percentage, of the farm income at the end of the year. Some of my Dad's brothers and sisters had purchased other farms Granddad owned, and a few farmed on Granddad's other properties. They also "farmed on the shares." Uncle Ernest and Aunt Grace were on the south farm, known as "the weaning farm." Uncle Coy and Aunt Myrtle were on a farm north of Granddad Hagan's house.

Our lives were changed by the move, but we soon settled into a routine again. My mother worked very hard to make sure my granddad was comfortable and his needs were met. One major change we experienced was gardening in a different location. My parents were quite meticulous about their large gardens. They spent more than a few evenings trying to plan the best way to utilize the new garden spot. Laundry was even different. The laundry was done in a shed located near the house. Vee and I quickly learned the most efficient way to get the laundry done.

Albert, Raycel and I shared a bedroom upstairs. My three sisters shared another large room upstairs. It was bigger than the one they had shared in our house. Raycel and I could hear them talking and giggling at night. Jessie had a sunny disposition and would make the younger girls laugh. They were all happy when they were together. My sisters were getting older and would fix each other's hair with curling irons. They were heated by putting them inside the chimney of a coal oil lamp. More than once they burned a finger or scorched their hair.

My grandfather slept on the first floor of the house, due to the stairs being difficult for him to manage, and because he seemed to be cold all the time. Our main source of heat was a wood stove located on the first floor. This house had a basement where we stored our jars of home canned foods.

While we were living there, Jessie and Albert left home to attend high school in Mercer, Missouri. Mom and Dad encouraged their children to get all of the education they desired. Many people in the 1920s felt that education beyond grade school was unnecessary. The school they attended was Mercer High School, because we were in the Mercer, Missouri School District. They rented a room because it was too far to walk or ride a horse each day to school. They returned home most weekends, in the summer and during the school holidays. Mom would send Jessie and Albert back to school with a sack of potatoes, milk and her home canned foods. I remember Albert saying he could buy a brain sandwich for five cents. I thought that was too much to pay for something so awful. When Albert was home, he would bunk in with Raycel and me on a cot. It was tight, but fun.

One of the things I enjoyed most growing up on a farm was riding the horses. Dad kept six or eight horses to use with wagons, plows, cultivators and other farm equipment and two or three riding horses. My brothers and I rode horses constantly as children. Horses are intelligent and have personalities much like people. Some are gentle and easily led, others are high spirited, or stubborn. Some horses refused to allow humans on their backs. My brothers and I would ride bareback, holding on tightly to their manes with our fingers. When my mother wasn't looking, I would practice doing tricks like standing up and trying to keep my balance while the horse was running. I had seen a stunt rider at the fair slide down one side of the horse and then go back up over the horse's back, then down the other side. I wanted to do that and tried many times before I was finally able to do it.

We had one horse that was ornery. He did not want to be ridden. Dad did not use him often, as it was too time-consuming to get him to cooperate. One day I decided I was going to ride him. I got astride of this large horse after many attempts. He looked a little wild-eyed at this point. He started running as fast as he could and I held on for dear life. He would stop suddenly, attempting to throw me off and then take off galloping again. I held on tighter with my knees and twisted his mane tightly around both of my hands. He tossed his head and even tried to buck me off. I slid back and forth on his back. I was exhausted, but had no intention of giving up. Unfortunately, neither did he. He ran toward Granddad's orchard, straight for an apple tree with low-growing branches. I got ready because I knew what he was going to do. When he got to the low branches, he ducked his head and tried to scrape me off of his back. I slid down to one side, just as I had practiced with the gentler horses. It worked and I was able to come back up on top. He turned around and did it again. Soon we were both exhausted and I had some bruises. He gave up and walked back to the barn area to drink water. I gratefully slid off his back. That was definitely the ride of my life.

One Sunday I rode a horse to church. She was a temperamental, racing type of horse. She was slender, long-legged, and very fast. As usual, I was riding bareback. I tied her up a long way from the other horses at Bethel Church because she was so lively. I waited until everyone left before I got on her back and started home to Granddad's house. Uncle Arthur and Aunt Gladys (Hagan) Finney lived between Bethel Church and Granddad's house. When we got close to the Finney house, I could see they had company and were sitting out in the yard. I was trying to hold the horse down to a short run. Uncle Arthur saw me coming, stood up, waved his arms and hat and yelled, "Let her run!" It scared the horse so badly she ran into the barn lot across from his house. I tried to turn her back to the road by the fence. When I made it to the corner of the fence next to the road, she jumped the fence and her front feet landed in the ditch. She almost fell. When she jumped over the fence, I slid back to her hips and held on to the reins. I squeezed my knees into her hipbones. I slid up around her neck when she hit the ditch. Somehow I was still hanging on. She stumbled around and started running up the road again. My cherished bill cap came off and I wanted to go back for it. I finally got my horse turned into the bank. I turned her around and started back, but she refused to go that way. I tied her to the fence and walked back for my cap. Uncle Arthur gave me my cap and apologized for spooking my horse.

My siblings and I walked to and from Hickory Grove School each day from Granddad Hagan's place. It was farther than it had been from our house. We also took a different route, going behind Granddad's house, through the fields toward the weaning farm. Eventually we got on a dirt road and followed it to Hickory Grove School. Every day we walked by a widow lady's home. She was an older, decrepit woman who had lived by herself for many years. One thing was funny to all of us. As we passed her property, she would feed her turkeys and call to them saying, "pee-dah, pee-dah." Vee, Reva, Raycel and I were thinking about that and we wrote a song:

Pee-dah, pee-dah,
There goes Mrs. Mitchell calling her turkeys,
Pee-dah, pee-dah,
Here come all her little "lurkeys,"
Pee-dah, pee-dah
There goes Mrs. Mitchell feeding her turkeys,
And they all sang pee-dah.

From childhood to our elder years, if Vee, Reva, Raycel or I wanted to make the others laugh, we would very quietly whisper "pee-dah."

The first time I drove a car was the summer we moved to Granddad Hagan's farm. My parents had stopped driving the 1919 Model T because there was something wrong with it. One day while my dad and older brothers were out in the fields working, I was able to get it running. I drove it even though it had only two tires, to our home farm several miles away. It was not a smooth ride, but I had a good time. When I got back home to Granddad's farm, I turned off the engine while I opened the shed doors. I was not able to get the car restarted. Because the car was not where it was supposed to be, my father knew I had driven it. He was not pleased about my adventure, but did not say anything to me.

My dad bought one of the first radios in our community. We set the radio on a table in the "front room," or the living room in Granddad's house. He enjoyed listening to the radio, but he had become quite hard of hearing. Mom recognized this and moved the radio next to his favorite chair. Neighbors, relatives and friends would come over to listen to it in the evenings. Soon several others began to get radios.

Static was a big problem in the country. After listening to the adults complain about the static, I decided to try an experiment. I found a box about the size of a cigar box, took some wire I found in the workshop and drilled a hole in the side of the box. I separated all the little wires then wound it up and down inside the box in a specific pattern of rows, running the wire out of the box on the other edge, and then twisted the wires back together. Next, I filled the box with melted paraffin. I attached the wire to the back of the radio. The static was gone. That was something that interested everyone who had a radio. My Uncle Ernest was fascinated by things like this and suggested I get a patent on it. He told me how to apply, so I wrote to Washington, D.C. to the U.S. Patent Office. I filled out the paperwork, but did not send it in. I did not have the money that was required to be sent in with the application.

On June 16, 1926, a devastating tornado hit our community. I was eleven years old. We hid in the basement on Granddad Hagan's farm. I peeked out of a small opening and saw a very large, wooden farm wagon fly through the air. It looked like it was sailing. I gained a great respect for the powerful forces of nature. Most of the damage was southwest of us toward Cainsville. After the tornado, my parents drove their newly repaired 1919 Model T Ford to Cainsville to see if they could help the people in need. Granddad and I rode with my parents. We saw a great deal of destruction in the countryside. We stopped to help an old woman sitting in a rocking chair in her front yard. The remains of her destroyed home were behind her. She was sitting in that rocking chair with a quilt thrown over her shoulders. My parents tried to talk to her, but she was barely able to speak. She said someone was coming to take her to the doctor. My mother tried to get her to come with us but the older lady shook her head. She kept rocking and staring into the distance. She was obviously in shock. She did not communicate any more. We reluctantly left and drove on to Cainsville.

Several times, Granddad talked to my parents after dinner about his property. My mother was unusually quiet while the men talked. I could tell she was concerned about the conversation. Granddad wanted to leave his property to his children in a way that it would be divided fairly. To do this, he planned to put one person's name on the deeds. He asked my Dad to be the one to distribute things after he passed away. My dad would not agree to this, as he was not the oldest, but rather the ninth child in the family that originally had thirteen children. Some of the family had moved far away and two had passed away by this time. Granddad was frustrated that Dad would not follow his wishes. He argued that Dad lived very close by and had farmed on his land with great care all of his life. My father only held ownership of the land he purchased from Uncle Jake, where he had built the wonderful red barn. Not many people dared to say no to my grandfather. This was the only time I knew of that Dad disagreed with Granddad. One evening my tiny and timid mother sat in front of Granddad, and in her gentle way, explained that this was not the right way to do things to keep peace in the family. It was obvious he held my mother in high regard and always spoke kindly to her. Granddad sat thoughtfully the rest of that evening. The next day he went to town and made arrangements for a capable older sibling, Uncle Jim, to take care of things and put his name on the paperwork. I could tell Dad and Mom were greatly relieved.

Once a year we would go to Lineville, Iowa, where Dad's sister and husband, Uncle John and Aunt Effie Rockey had a clothing and dry goods store. We would buy fabric for the girls' dresses and the boys' shirts, thread and buttons, overalls, shoes, and socks. Leather shoes and boots cost between two and four dollars a pair. With a family of nine people needing clothing and shoes, the cost added up. Due to this, we wore hand-me-downs from our older sisters and brothers. Getting hand-me-downs was a wonderful event. When a garment was too worn to be handed down or repaired, Mom used it to make quilts and potholders, saving the buttons to be used on another garment. Mom sewed our shirts and all the dresses for herself and the girls, as well as aprons. My mother wore aprons over her dresses every day, except for church on Sunday. I never saw my mother wear anything other than a dress. She would occasionally purchase yarn and make knitted hats and mittens for us to wear in the cold winters. This annual excursion was very exciting for us all. Everyone looked forward to this shopping trip and for the opportunity to see our family members who lived in Lineville. We could have shopped elsewhere, but we wanted to give our business to one of Dad's favorite sisters. While we were there, Raycel and I would visit a local furrier to sell the stretched pelts from the animals we had trapped.

We always enjoyed sharing a meal with Uncle John and Aunt Ef. She was friendly and made us feel at ease. She had the gift of hospitality. There was a lot of laughing and talking, as we tried to catch up on all of the families' lives. Their son, Ray Rockey was the same age as Albert. They also had an older son and daughter. Aunt Ef was an excellent cook and often prepared things we did not normally get, because she had access to everything in their store. It was a treat for us to see them.

Before we left town, we would stop to see my great-uncle, Jake Hagan. Dad had purchased our farm from him. He lived in Lineville during his retirement years. His wife divorced him in 1913 and his children abandoned him because they felt he was too great a burden on them. My father was very kind to Uncle Jake. He spoke gently to him and listened to what he had to say. Sometimes my mother would take him something she had baked or a newspaper with local stories of interest to him. My parents felt sorry for him. He had few visitors and was in poor health. He lived in a house where people helped care for his daily needs. Raycel, Reva, Darrell and I stood behind my parents, because we never knew what Uncle Jake was trying to say to us. Dad could understand his speech, but I could rarely understand what he said. Our visits were a great blessing to him. When Granddad was feeling up to the trip, he would also go to see his daughter, Effie and his brother, Jake. After many years of poor health, Uncle Jake passed away in 1925. He had lived alone or with the assistance of caretakers for twelve years.

We would often gather in the evening for parties at someone's home. The adults and youth played various games. We played a card game called Rook, checkers, Chinese checkers and Carom on a wooden game board. In warm weather we were likely to have a game of horseshoes in the yard. My dad was excellent at pitching a horseshoe, often scoring a "ringer." These "get-togethers" involved large quantities of popcorn and apples, which I still love. My dad was a champion checkers player. People of all ages would come over to play those games. In addition to a radio, we had a graphophone that played cylindrical disks. A graphophone is an improved version of the phonograph. Albert had an excellent singing voice that everyone loved to hear. We would persuade him to sing with the graphophone or the piano.

Baseball was another favorite pastime. My father was an outstanding pitcher. He taught all of his sons how to play ball. I worked at pitching because Dad told me that a "southpaw" pitcher could usually strike out right-handed batters. People would often come by our house and ask Dad to pitch a game for their team. Sometimes those games were quite a distance away in other towns. Raycel and I both loved to go to ball games and played every chance we were given. Like Dad, Raycel was a very talented ball player. For a few summers, Bethel Church had a team. The Hagan boys were frequently members of the team.

Jesse Delores Hagan Lafollette and Lawrence Lafollette on their wedding day: November 25, 1926

My pretty, petite sister, Jessie met a man named Lawrence Lafollette. After courting for several years, they decided to get married. Lawrence was a wonderful fellow. He fit right in with our easygoing family. Mother, Jessie, Reva and Vee made her wedding dress. The girls also made things for her hope chest, such as embroidered tea towels and pillowcases.

Their wedding was held at Bethel Church on November 25, 1926, with our sister, Vee serving as maid of honor. My big sisters were both beautiful. Vee had dark hair and large expressive eyes, while Jessie had curly blonde hair and blue eyes. All of us took part in the wedding. Albert came home from high school for the event. It was exciting for our first sibling to get married. After their wedding, they lived in Leon, Iowa. In a few months we heard the news that Lawrence and Jessie were expecting a child. This would be the first grandbaby for my parents, Ross and Pearle. There was a lot of excitement and preparations for the little one. The girls sewed tiny baby clothes while guessing what Jessie and Lawrence would name their baby.

Jessie had a difficult time during the pregnancy and delivery. My mother wanted Jessie to see Dr. Duffy, our family doctor. Lawrence's parents insisted she go to their doctor in Iowa. Her doctor in Iowa was out of town the night Jessie went into labor. She was in hard labor for two days. She was petite like Mom and the baby was breech. Lawrence had trouble finding help for Jessie. A midwife came and delivered the baby boy and tried to stop Jessie from hemorrhaging.

She packed Jessie with cotton. Dr. Duffy was finally called in to see Jessie. When he got there, she had bled so much she was near death. On September 19, 1927, both Jessie and her baby son passed away. This shocking news caused tremendous sorrow in our home. My sister Vee was affected by Jessie's death for the remainder of her life. Less than a year after we celebrated Jessie's wedding, we laid Jessie, with her baby son in her arms, to rest in Bethel Cemetery. This was hard on everyone, but the fact she had given her heart to Jesus and was baptized assured us we would see her in heaven one day.

In 1927, at the age of twelve, I attended my first boy-girl party at Uncle Jim Hagan's house. They lived in the first house north of Freedom Church. We played a game called Spin the Bottle. There were many from the Hagan family attending, so when you took your turn and it landed on a cousin, you got to spin again. The kids would run off laughing and go outside to kiss. I took my turn and the bottle pointed to an older girl. I had never kissed anyone except my mom and grandmother. I went outside with her, took her hand and ran her around the house as fast as I could. She laughed until she had to stop to catch her breath. I was thankful she never told the others why we were gone so long, and that I had not kissed her. We also played a game called Imagination. We were asked, "If you could have anything in the world, what it would be?"

"World peace" was mentioned. When it was my turn, I said I thought I'd just take a little more gravy. Everyone laughed, especially Reva.

Following Albert's example, Vee started high school in Mercer in 1928. She lived with a family we knew there. She worked cooking, babysitting, and cleaning house to earn her bed and meals. She worked very hard for this family and never missed her classes. Vee was diligent in everything, as though she was working for the Lord. I admired her dependability. Our family greatly missed her when she went to high school.

My Granddad Hagan experienced many issues related to aging. He was nearing eighty years old, walked with a cane, and tolerated a hearing loss. Each day seemed to bring new aches and pains. He was not fond of doctors and preferred to suffer in silence. My mother doted on him, cooking special dishes and buying liniment for his knees. He kept going on with a smile, no matter how he felt or what the weather was like.

Before his eightieth birthday, Granddad decided to plan a trip. Not just a trip, but a really big trip. He decided to go west to visit family members who were spread out around the country. I remember that nearly all of the extended family tried to dissuade him from going, but true to his character, Granddad Robert was firm in his decisions. In the late 1920s, this trip would involve careful planning. He got a train schedule and began to plan an itinerary. I can still see him sitting with train schedules and maps at the dining room table, carefully plotting the best routes. He wrote letters to the family members he planned to visit. My mother and Reva helped him with this task. Descendants of his beloved sister, Belinda Frank, lived in Boise, Idaho. His nephew, Charles Hagan, whom he had fondly known as "Shadow" in Pennsylvania (son of John Henry Hagan), was living in Los Angeles, California, with his wife. His daughter, Fleet (Fleeta) Hagan Shirley was residing near Anton, Colorado, and his oldest daughter, (Eliza) Jane Hagan Dunn was living on a farm close to Hutchison Kansas. They wrote Granddad Robert letters, telling him about their lives and the wonderful places they lived. Granddad was the last surviving sibling in his family after his younger brother, Jake passed in 1925. It was easy to understand the desire to visit his remaining family. Granddad was a devoted family man, accustomed to having a large family surrounding him. He was excited about his trip.

When the big day finally arrived, Granddad Robert was up early. My mother packed a box of food for him, including fried chicken and some of her sugar cookies. My dad took him to the train station in Princeton, Missouri, and loaded his belongings on the train. He told my dad he could not help thinking back to his youth to another adventure, nearly sixty years before. Robert was again going to leave everything familiar to explore new and exciting places. He was anxious to go west, but this time, not to start a new life. He planned to return to his beautiful Missouri home in a few months. He told his son, Ross goodbye and settled into his comfortable seat. He realized this train ride was an easier way to travel westward than the wagon train expedition in his youth. His first stop was Colorado.

We heard about Granddad when he visited my aunt, Fleet Hagan Shirley in Colorado. Aunt Fleet wrote that my double cousin, Ovid grew quite attached to Granddad and would not leave his side. They had a wonderful visit. Ovid reminisced about this visit with me many years later. He related that his family had moved to Colorado from Oklahoma, and all of them were delighted to have family visiting them. It had been a very long time since they had seen any of their family. Ovid and I were lifelong friends, even into our retirement years.

Granddad visited other relations west of Colorado, family members of his brother, John Henry Hagan; and then traveled to California to be with his nephew Charles, the oldest son of John Henry. Charles was about four years old when Granddad left Pennsylvania to move to Missouri, promising Charles he would see him again. Charles and his wife Sarah, now in their sixties, lived in Los Angeles County, California. In a short letter to Mom and Dad, Granddad said he enjoyed the warm temperatures in California, and was thankful to see Charles again, but he was not functioning at full strength. Due to this difficulty, he shortened his stay in California, and went on to Kansas.

He spent the Thanksgiving and Christmas season with his oldest child, Jane Hagan Dunn and her family, on their farm in Abbyville, near Hutchison, Kansas.

Her letters to my parents indicated they had a very nice Thanksgiving feast, but Granddad was unusually quiet. A few days before Christmas, Granddad admitted he was in pain. Aunt Jane took him to see a doctor on the 23rd of December. He was diagnosed with an enlarged prostate, cysts in his urinary tract, and hardening of the arteries. By New Year's Eve, something was terribly wrong. Robert could not urinate. Much to his dismay, the doctor said he needed to put in a catheter immediately, as uremic poisoning was beginning to set in. Despite the family's encouragement, and perhaps due to modesty, he flatly refused to allow a catheter to be used. We never understood why he refused medical treatment. He passed away on January 2, 1928. Granddad Robert did not get to complete his journey as planned. Arteriosclerosis, which is better known as atherosclerosis, was the official cause of death listed on his death certificate. Secondary was an enlarged prostate and cystitis of the urinary tract. Granddad Robert was transported home by train and laid to rest in Bethel cemetery, beside his wife and my grandmother, Sarah.

Aunt Jane rode the train home with her father's casket. As she sat at my parent's dining table, she recounted the last days of Granddad Robert's life. I listened and quietly observed the reactions of my mom and dad. Aunt Jane was heartbroken that he had refused medical treatment that could have saved his life. I saw my dad put his head in his hands, silently grieving the passing of his father and best friend. I saw tears roll down all their faces. They talked far into the night, reminiscing about my grandparents' lives, and being raised in such a large family. Over the next few days, our little home was full of family members, laughing, crying, and remembering stories from days gone by. Dad was close to his siblings and I heard him share encouraging words with them about being reunited on the other side. The funeral was at Bethel Church. The main thing I remember is the crowd was large and the weather was freezing cold. After the service, many relatives were in our kitchen and parlor, having a reunion far into the night.

In the span of just fifteen months, we lost three family members; Jessie, her baby boy and now Granddad Hagan. My parents carried this sadness in their hearts, but continued to rise at four every morning and work until bedtime. They did their best without slacking or complaining about the situation. I often heard them pray and talk to the Lord. I appreciated their example most when I was older and reminisced about their lives. They taught me two important life lessons. We have to give everything to God in prayer, and keep on living, even when our hearts are broken. And we should cherish those we love while they are with us and after they pass into eternity. Family ties are never broken. Life goes on after hardships.

Chapter 11
MOOSE MONEY

After we moved back to our farm, one of the first things Dad did was paint the barn and had a man talented in painting carefully letter the name of his farm on it. To me, it seemed Dad knew how to do everything and I was grateful he wanted to pass those skills to his sons. We learned by working alongside him. He could create something he needed out of nothing. He could turn a piece of scrap metal into a gate latch or make a needed part for farm machinery. I wanted to be just like him. This mindset, to make something we needed out of nothing, made us all overcomers in the years ahead.

My siblings and I were growing up. Albert changed schools, and graduated from Princeton High School. He was an excellent student and was on the debate team. His teachers encouraged him to attend college. This was discussed around our supper table many times. Dad and Mom wanted Albert to have a good education, but paying for it was a concern. Albert took a teaching position at a nearby country school, called Cavanaugh, and saved his money for college tuition.

In 1928, I was just thirteen, and attended services at Bethel. Raycel, Reva and I were in the young teenage Sunday school class. Darrell was in the children's Sunday school class. The teenagers filled the two front rows of seats. There was a high church attendance in those days. Some of the people who attended were: Wayne and Mildred Hollcroft, Pauline Sparagur, Lloyd Larason, Roger Dunn, Hubert, Avis, Lloyd, Fay, Carl, and Ferril Hagan, Gladys and Arthur Eastin, Clell and Lois Dunn and their family, Margaret Parsons, Leo and Erma Dunn and their children, Bert and Nell Robins with their children, Ernest Dale and Laura Estaline, Ralph and Opal Dorland with their children, Maurice,

Clarie Jo, Max, Merrill, and Betty, and Mervil and Veta Hagan with their first baby, Ovid Don. Most of those people were related to me.

A favorite activity of the children, and my dad, was the ice cream socials held in the church yard. We had large freezers of various flavors of homemade ice cream, made with real cream. My favorite was peach. Other desserts were brought in to go with the ice cream. What a wonderful way to spend a summer day!

Raycel and I were now Dad's main help on the farm. Darrell and Reva had taken charge of the laundry day duties. Raycel worked side-by-side with Dad, while I went to Hickory Grove School with Reva, and Darrell. Raycel had turned into a very strong and hard-working young man. He loved farming and wanted to follow in Dad's footsteps. He was also blessed with a great sense of humor. I always enjoyed working with him.

Albert wrote letters to the Northwest Missouri Normal School, in Maryville. He filled out an application to apply for scholarships. He took correspondence classes while he taught school. Later he attended classes while working in Maryville. He rented a room from a family, as he had done in high school. He was very successful in his college coursework. He was also recognized for his singing talent and was asked to join a quartet. Albert made it through college by teaching one year and then attending college one year, living on the money he made teaching.

My mom had a small cream pitcher shaped like a moose. The head of the moose had a full set of horns. The mouth of the moose had an opening to pour out the cream. This had been a wedding gift to my parents in September of 1907. Mother kept the cream pitcher on top of the kitchen cabinet. She kept a little of her egg money in it for small emergencies.

When Albert was a freshman in college, he came home for a visit. The quartet he sang with would sing and give testimonies at churches in various communities. They even sang on a radio show in Iowa. They needed no instruments, singing a cappella in perfect harmony. Albert told Mother he needed money to travel with them. His friend, Bill was the tenor. He had told Albert they might need fifteen dollars. Reva and I were shocked when she pulled twenty dollars out of the moose and gave it to him. That was about the most money we had ever seen. Raycel, Vee, Reva and I thought Albert was an amazing brother and looked up to him. Mom was proud that Albert was singing for the Lord.

One day Albert came home from college wearing new shoes and fancy trousers. This was what he wore when he sang with the quartet. Raycel and I were near one of the ponds working in our denim overalls. Of course the cattle went in and out of the water. Albert came and told us he was home for a day or two. He sat on a stump as we talked and teased each other. When he stood up to return to the house, he had a little dirt on the seat of his new pants. He asked Raycel and me to take his ankles and pull him across an area of clean grass to get the dirt off of his pants. Raycel laughed and teased him about his fancy pants, but we quickly agreed to help him out. Albert sat down and Raycel and I each grabbed one of his legs. About fifteen feet ahead of us was a fresh cow pile. Raycel looked at it and then at me. We never said a word, but started running as fast as we could go, dragging Albert behind us. We took him straight through the cow pile before we stopped. We collapsed on the ground, laughing, and thankfully, Albert thought it was hilarious as well. We did help him clean up afterwards. There was never a boring moment around my brothers.

Chapter 12

THE WINDS OF CHANGE

When the Great Depression started after the Wall Street collapse in October of 1929, everything seemed to fall apart. Life changed suddenly and dramatically for everyone. After the stock market crashed, many businesses closed, or laid off workers. We heard about it on the radio and in the newspapers. I did not fully understand the impact of what was happening. I was surprised that people in New York were leaping off of buildings to take their lives. We were all greatly affected by the situation. Within a few months, many people across the nation lost their jobs. Many businesses closed their doors. The banks in Lineville, Saline, and Pleasanton, which were close to our farm, went under and closed their doors within a period of about two years. Some people lost all of the money they had in those banks. My Granddad Hagan had served on the board of directors for each of these banks. Although he had some financial concerns before his death, I was glad for his sake he was in heaven now and did not have to experience this terrible situation.

Suddenly no one had money. Some conditions were worse in farming areas, where commodity prices plunged quickly. By late 1930, just twelve months after the stock market crash, a steady decline in the world economy had set in, and did not reach bottom until 1933. For us it became impossible to sell what we raised on Dad's farm. Every farmer struggled with low prices all through the 1920s, but after October of 1929 things began to go downhill in a hurry for all of us. Most families did not have money to buy the things they needed, not even food. I never once heard my parents complain. They taught us to make do with what we had and never give up.

In the early 1930s, prices dropped so low that many farmers went bankrupt and lost their farms. One day Dad was outside the barn he had built, working with cattle, when a man wearing a suit and a fancy hat stopped by. He was from the bank where Dad had the mortgage on our farm. I was nearby helping Dad and was able to hear every word they said. The man demanded payment on the farm mortgage. Dad and Mom were late on their annual payment. Dad repeatedly told the man he would make the payment as soon as he was able, but this seemed to make the banker more assertive. Dad stood quietly for a moment and then said, "If you cannot wait, I guess you can have the deed to our farm." One look at my father told me he was devastated. The banker suddenly said, "No! I do not want or need another farm deed, I need operating cash." Dad calmly repeated that he would keep his word and would make the payment as quickly as he was able. I wished that I had the money to give my dad. I prayed to the Lord to help my parents so they could keep their farm. It was some time before Dad was able to make the payment. From time to time he would take a dollar or two to the bank, to show them he was trying to pay his debt.

The price for a bushel of corn fell to just eight to ten cents. Some farmers became angry and wanted the government to step in to keep their families in their homes. We heard on the radio that a mob of frustrated farmers in Le Mars, Iowa went in and carried the judge out of the courtroom. They took him into the country and tried to make him promise that he would not take any more cases that would cause a family to lose their farm. When he refused, they threatened to hang him. Although they did not actually hang him, it must have frightened him tremendously. The governor of Iowa called out the National Guard to round up the mob and put them in jail.

In some ways, farmers were better off than city dwellers. More people were out of work than were working. We could produce much of our own food, while city residents could not. Almost all farm families raised large gardens with vegetables and canned fruit from their orchards. They had milk and cream from their dairy cattle. Chickens supplied meat and eggs. We still had to buy salt, sugar and flour. We bought flour and sugar in fifty-pound sacks and baked our own bread. In our family, Mom and my sisters made clothing out of the printed cloth from flour and feed sacks. We learned how to get by with very little money. We still had to pay taxes and our farm mortgage payment to the bank in cash, and cash was in short supply. Times were tough on every farm.

When I was fifteen, and my brother Raycel was nineteen, we had an interesting encounter. It was October 1930 and we were home working together on the farm. It was almost one year after the stock market crash that caused the Great Depression. A man we did not know came by Dad's farm and needed water for his Model A Ford Coupe. It was overheating. Raycel and I were glad to help him and did not hesitate to pump water for him, carry it to the car and pour it in the radiator. He was friendly, chatting while we waited for the radiator to cool. He thanked us before he went on his way. Later we learned he had just

The winds of change

robbed the Citizens Bank of Saline, taking $2,360 from cashier Roy Finney. He had pulled a gun and forced Roy to give him the money from his cash drawer and the vault. We had no idea the friendly man had just robbed a bank. From our farm, he went to Mercer, Missouri. We kept listening for more news about the robbery. The money and his gun must have been in the car while we chatted with him. He was finally caught and arrested in Kansas City two months later. Raycel and I discussed this several times, because he seemed like a very nice man. The economic collapse caused people to do things out of desperation they probably would not have considered a few months earlier. I learned a life lesson about indebtedness. The Bible is very clear concerning indebtedness in Proverbs 22:26-27. "Do not be a man who strikes hands in pledge or puts up security for debts; if you lack the means to pay, your very bed will be snatched from under you." Not long after this, the bank in Saline closed its doors.

Many times I have had a yearning to buy a farm. I loved the challenge of farming as a business. The debt that came with a farm purchase was so unsettling to me; I could never make that financial commitment.

Occasionally people we did not know would stop by our house looking for a meal. Even though we were far from any sizeable town, the number of people coming by started to increase. Mom would always feed them, and allow them to wash up at our pump. She felt sorry for anyone who did not have the necessities of life. She prayed for them after they were gone. Dad and Mom had compassionate hearts. They gave to others when they had needs of their own. I grew up thinking I should have this kind of heart.

Although many things were changed by the terrible financial issues during the Great Depression, in my community, we maintained a simple social life and kept close contact with those around us. In 1930, when I was fifteen, nearly fifty of my friends and family members gathered in A.D. Campbell's timber, just behind the first house west of the Freedom Church. Asa, Letha, Margaret and Beth Campbell had a big party. The young folks from the area were all invited. We had a bonfire and roasted wieners and marshmallows. We played games such as Skip-to-my-Lou and danced to our own singing. Those attending were the Campbell girls, me and two of my siblings, Reva and Raycel, Mr. and Mrs. Lloyd Larason, Fay, Hubert, and Lloyd Hagan, Joe, Francis, and Pauline Sparagur, Leland Larason, Junior, Wilda, and Bessie Bagley, Maurice and Clarence Griffin, Lester Hagan, Mildred and Wayne Hollcroft, Vernon Nichols, Opal Craig, George and Anna Wolford, Laura and Elsa Seymour, Daisy and Elmer Norris, Kenneth Helton, Ray Pace, Julia, Emma Lois, and Manford Leeper, Pauline Hart, Velma Ceradsky, Herbert Dunn, Thelma Trembly, Guy and Basil Simpson, and Delbert, Harley, and Harold Flanagan. Many of these young people were my cousins.

As far back as I can remember, the Hagan clan always had an annual reunion at the end of summer. One Sunday, in August of 1930, about 150 relatives and friends of the Dunn and Hagan families gathered at Bethel Church for a family reunion and basket dinner. We sat on quilts and blankets on the lawn to eat our lunch. Because everyone was poor and concerned about their finances, the fellowship and love of family was appreciated even more that summer.

Bethel Church

By 1931, Dad had tried to sell his hogs and sheep for many months, to no avail. Before the Depression, hogs would sell for approximately $100 a head, depending on the size and quality. Suddenly, they were worth nothing. The livestock became a liability as they must be fed, and would not bring in cash income. We needed cash to make the farm payments and pay our taxes. Finally Dad was able to get a man to come out and look at the livestock. When Dad took him to see the sheep, I tagged along to see what would transpire. The man looked at Dad and said, "I don't want sheep at all. I cannot sell them in Kansas City. There is no market for them anywhere." Dad took him to see the registered hogs. They were almost bigger than what was desirable. The man told Dad he really did not want the hogs either, due to current market conditions. A long discussion ensued about the hard financial times in our country. The man finally told my father, "I don't want the lambs but I will give you fifty cents a head for the hogs." After haggling back and forth, my father sold him the hogs for one dollar a head if he would take all forty lambs for nothing. Dad sold just over a hundred hogs and forty sheep for about one hundred dollars. My easygoing father took it all in stride and said he was thankful he had been able to get rid of them.

Ross & Pearle Hagan

Chapter 13

BEING AN OPTIMIST– NO MATTER WHAT!

In the spring of 1931, Reva and I finished eighth grade in the little one-room school, Hickory Grove. We had walked about two miles to school and back each day. There were no school busses in those days. We both wanted to go to high school in town, but most country children could not go because they had no transportation to take them there, or the finances to live away from home.

In 1931, the Depression had continued for two years and most families were having severe financial problems. Many local farmers, and farmers across the nation, had lost their farms. My parents were hanging on by the grace of God. Although we were all living in grinding poverty, I did not recognize myself as poor. Poverty was a normal part of life for everyone we knew. In retrospect, I realize no one ever said we were poor. Everyone was in the same boat financially. It was understood without discussion that extended family members helped each other all they could.

During the month of July, Mr. George Tumbleson, the vocational agriculture teacher from the high school in Princeton, Missouri, held a meeting in Saline for area farmers. My father and I went to this meeting. After the meeting ended, Mr. Tumbleson talked privately to Dad and me. I told him I just finished the eighth grade and hoped to go to high school. He told me about his four-year program and said I should come to Princeton High School and take vocational agriculture classes. It sounded very interesting to me. My father explained we were in the Mercer, Missouri school district, so that was where I needed to attend. Mr. Tumbleson said if I wanted to get into a vocational agriculture program, I needed to go to school in Princeton. I was excited when he looked at Dad and said, "If you pay tuition, Raymond can come to Princeton."

Later my parents told me they could not afford to send me to Princeton, but I could attend Mercer for free. I understood the situation, but was very disappointed. Over the next two weeks, my family had many discussions about high school. My sister Vee had finished her junior year at Mercer, and was dating a handsome young man, Bill Alley. His family had moved from Mercer to Princeton. I think this encouraged Vee to say she wanted to go to Princeton her senior year. My other sister, Reva was a year younger than me, but she was also ready for high school. We learned that my first cousin, Lester Hagan, who had graduated from Hickory Grove School with Reva and me, also wanted to go to Princeton. I tried to come up with a way to earn the tuition. I had trapped animals all winter to sell their skins. Sadly, there was hardly anyone interested in buying them now. Reva, Vee and I could share a room, and we were willing to work if we could find jobs. Uncle Ernest, Lester's father, said he would pay for Lester's part of the rent if he could stay with us. He felt it would be good for Lester to live with us since Vee was older and very responsible. My parents somehow came up with enough money to get us all in school the first semester, but we needed to earn our tuition fees and living expenses thereafter.

After a great deal of effort, my parents located an eighty-two-year-old widow in Princeton, willing to rent a room in her home. I suspect she needed the money to supplement her income. It was a large room on the front of her house, with a wood-heating stove and a kerosene cooking stove in it. It was a big savings to have all four of us share one room. This room was furnished with two large beds with a sheet hanging between them. Cousin Lester and I were on one side of the sheet and Vee and Reva were on the other side. The bathroom was down the hallway and shared with the landlord. An inside bathroom was new to us and a wonderful luxury. This was home for my sisters, our cousin, Lester, and me from September to the following May. We had a charge account at the grocery store where we bought small amounts of food. My parents paid the charge account until we could get jobs. We purchased as little food as possible so we would not create a big bill.

Due to the hilly, dirt roads and the distance to travel, we seldom went home. We literally kept from starving because we received help from Vee's future in-laws, Mr. and Mrs. Alley. Sometimes they would invite us all over to play our favorite card game, Rook. She would make popcorn and candy. What a treat. When we did go home to the farm, we brought home-canned food and potatoes back with us.

During that time, a teenage boy we became acquainted with at school, had a crush on Reva, my shy and pretty little sister. His father was a local dairy farmer who delivered milk in town. We sent Reva to the porch when the boy delivered our milk because he would give us extra milk and butter to impress Reva.

We looked forward to letters from home. Darrell would write to us often. The house must have seemed quiet with only one brother left. Darrell got a bad case of chicken pox after we had been home for Christmas. Thankfully, the three of us did not catch them.

Everything went well my first year in high school due to the efforts of my remarkable older sister, Vee, and the good Lord. We prayed over every meal and Vee made sure we attended the Princeton Methodist Church every Sunday.

I tried out for football as a freshman. Each student was required to furnish their own equipment. I had no equipment, so I looked for cast off gear in the locker rooms. I found shirts and pants, but shoes were difficult to find because my feet are short and wide. I found an old pair of football shoes in the trash. They were about three sizes too large and had cleats that felt like nails sticking into my feet. In spite of their condition, I used them. I got along well in football. We had many practice sessions and games to play. With my determination and speed, I could go through the line during practice. At first I did not get to play often in practice, but the coaches allowed me to play more frequently as the season progressed. One day the coach put me in the backfield with the team kicking off. A muscular quarterback caught the ball. I ran through the line to meet him head on. When he went right, I went to the right. When he went left, I went to the left. We continued until he was directly in front of me. I was scared. I was a freshman, he was a senior; but I was determined to finish what I went down the field to do. When he turned right to go around me, I tucked my shoulder and hit him below the knees. After we connected, he turned a complete flip-flop in the air. This play was over before the other players made it down the field. It made a compelling impression on them.

That evening I went to the drugstore. The quarterback and three of the other first string players were drinking a Coke. The quarterback looked at me and said, "This is the guy that flipped me up in the air head-over-heels!" I was relieved he said it with a smile on his face and was not mad at me! He was glad to see a young freshman willing to play hard. The coach began to put me in the games more often, but that created a problem, because those awful shoes were tearing up my feet. I quit playing football after my freshman year because I lacked money to buy the proper equipment.

We had a wonderful first year in high school. Vee was instrumental in getting us started on the right foot in school, and learning to live away from our families. She helped us with homework, and made sure we ate something for dinner every night. She worked for a family with children to earn a little money. Lester and I did yard work every opportunity we could find. We mowed the yards using push mowers that belonged to the homeowners, raked leaves and split firewood. The money was used for tuition and food. Reva managed to get a job babysitting. By the end of the year, I was blessed to get a better paying job with a local dairy farmer. It was very hard work, but I was able to put money back for tuition for the following year. We survived financially because we were extremely frugal. Not one of us spent a penny unless it was for food, tuition or rent.

My favorite part of high school was the vocational agriculture class. Mr. Tumbleson was an excellent teacher. In one class we were required to make a huge wall chart showing the stock market's daily changes. He had a great interest in agriculture economics. This in turn made me excited about agriculture economics. I learned a good deal in all of my classes, but what I thought was most important, I learned from Mr. Tumbleson. I kept that stock market chart current for many years. During this time I read the newspapers, and Mr. Tumbleson taught current events, especially about the collapse of the European economy in April of 1931. This was something I could not imagine was possible. The Great Depression became even worse. President Hoover called for a suspension of international debt payments, which saved the international banking system from a complete collapse. With foreign trade at a standstill, prices for U.S. manufactured goods and farm products fell even further, and American industries began laying off more workers. Through the eyes of my wise teacher, I was beginning to understand the terrible situation we were living in.

Vocational agriculture students were encouraged to join an organization called FFA, which stands for Future Farmers of America. The FFA had regular meetings after school. Each FFA member was required to work on a project related to the agriculture industry. The project I selected was raising a registered Hereford beef cow and calf. I had to maintain records on each animal. I kept track of feed, weights, wellness checks and much more. I was required to show them at the local fair. During the second FFA meeting at Princeton High School, we elected officers. I was shocked to be elected sentinel as a "greenhand." Officers were usually upperclassmen.

Lester Hagan, my high-spirited cousin, did not share my love of learning. In fact, he did not like high school at all. He told us after Christmas break that he had no plans to return to high school the following year. His parents, Uncle Ernest and Aunt Grace were farming on "the weaning farm." Aunt Grace seemed frail, and was sick a great deal of the time. Their young daughters, Wilma and Lillian, were helping run their home. Lester was needed to work alongside his father on the farm. These three cousins and I were good friends as children and all through our lives. Wilma was one of the kindest people I have ever known.

We were all proud when Vee graduated that year. She had worked very hard to make it through high school. Her grades were excellent. She wanted to attend college, but again finances were a difficulty. She took a teaching position at Upper Tennessee School, a one-room country school located northwest of Princeton, Missouri. She also began taking correspondence classes from Maryville Teacher's College. God continued to make a way for her when there seemed to be no way.

Vee, Raymond and Reva at Princeton High School on Vee's graduation day. 1932

In May, Vee, Reva and I went home and worked on the farm during the summer. Lester did the same. We worked hard to repay the loving generosity Mom and Dad had shown by helping us go to high school. It was good to be with Darrell and Raycel again. Raycel was turning into a strong and handsome young man. He was my father's right hand man with the farm work. Darrell was intelligent and quickly learned how to do anything by watching someone else. He attended Hickory Grove School. Both of my brothers were learning to play the guitar. This made great entertainment in the evenings with Reva accompanying them on the piano. Sometimes Dad joined the musicians on his harmonica.

In late summer there was an event we all looked forward to. The entire family, even Albert, went to the county fair. I showed my Herefords as part of my FFA project. Everyone in the family entered something to be judged at the fair. Mom entered home-canned fruits and vegetables. One of my sisters took an item she had quilted. Raycel entered a registered Hereford bull. This was an event we always looked forward to attending as a family. We brought home several blue ribbons that year.

In the fall of 1932, Reva and I began our sophomore year in high school. My parents found an upstairs room for us to rent, in a very old house that was owned by another elderly widow. It was a much smaller room and thankfully the rent was less as well. Reva was fortunate to get a job in the home of a family doing household chores, cleaning, washing dishes and doing laundry. We survived by earning money any way we could and eating an extremely limited diet. We no longer had help from our parents. They were in a financial crisis, trying to hang on to their farm. For Reva and me, food was scarce and occasionally nonexistent. All of the high school students went home for lunch. Reva and I would meet at our room and eat a few bites of whatever was available. Sometimes nothing was available except water. One week we had only home-canned tomatoes. Several weeks we had only sorghum and no bread. We were constantly hungry. Our jobs enabled us to pay the rent and tuition, but little else. Reva and I did not have money for a trip to the farm to get canned fruits and vegetables. One day, after a few weeks on our sorghum diet, Reva and I came back to our room to a wonderful surprise. Someone had left a large plate of homemade rolls on our table. They were still warm and delicious. We had not enjoyed a feast like that in a very long time. We decided our bread-baking angel from God had to be our landlord. She had no idea we were getting weak from hunger. We prayed blessings over that dear lady. Our lives went well until it got cold. Suddenly we realized there was no heat upstairs. We were so cold we wore our coats, hats, and all the clothes we could at night.

Our high school classes were wonderful. I loved vocational agriculture class and was disappointed that Mr. Tumbleson had moved away. He took a teaching position near the area where he grew up, in south Missouri. My new teacher was dedicated to building the program. His name was Mr. G.K. Arney. The students soon respected him. FFA continued to be very important to me. This year I was elected treasurer. My responsibilities included keeping records of the FFA checking account. This was another excellent experience for me. I learned to write checks, make deposits and balance the checkbook. Those skills helped me greatly all through life.

Reva learned secretarial skills in a few of her classes. In a shorthand class she learned how to take notes quickly. Shorthand looked like hieroglyphics to me. We were both required to take classes in English, math, history and science. We had a lot more homework that year.

The United States presidential election was held in November of 1932. Mr. Roosevelt blamed President Hoover for the Depression and the worsening economy. I did not understand how he could be responsible for the stock market crash. Mr. Roosevelt promised economic recovery with a "New Deal" for the American people. Everyone wanted economic recovery. Franklin Roosevelt won by a landslide and became our new president. Even though the high school students were not old enough to vote, they celebrated the elections. Everyone wanted our nation to return to better financial times. The election brought hope for a brighter future.

I tried out for the basketball team during my sophomore year. Once again, I lacked appropriate clothing or shoes. Although I was short, I was fast and fairly good at scoring points. A difficult problem soon became apparent. I had to deal with prejudice. The other players, known as "town kids," were from Princeton. "Country kids" like me were considered inferior. The players who were raised in town would ignore me when they passed the ball, even when I was open and directly under the basket. I did not continue with that sport. I determined to find better ways to use my energies.

Reva and I finished our sophomore year together. We were much thinner in May than in September, but we survived. We were excited to go home for the summer and be surrounded by our loving family. We could not wait to have Mom's fried chicken and cream gravy. I had especially missed her gravy. We worked hard all summer, in the fields, gardens, and anywhere a helping hand was needed. I felt blessed to able to eat often, picking fruit right off the trees when I got hungry. Although life was difficult financially for my parents, the farm did provide food. Never before had I appreciated our gardens and orchard as much as I did now.

Something was new at the family farm. With other area farmers, Dad helped run REA electric lines nineteen miles, the first in the county, to the Hagan farm. Electricity was going to change our country lifestyle in many ways.

Vee attended classes at Maryville Teachers College that summer, using money she had saved during her first year as a teacher. The elementary students adored Vee and she became attached to them. She planned to return to her teaching position in the fall, while taking correspondence classes from Maryville Teachers College.

In the fall of 1933, my youngest brother Darrell began his last year at Hickory Grove School. Reva and I began our junior year at Princeton High School. I was proud of Reva when she got a job with a beauty operator. Her duties included washing and pin curling hair with bobby pins, and cleaning the shop. Part of her payment was a room to sleep in and a little money for tuition. I was able to get a job on a dairy farm just four miles outside of Princeton. I lived with my employer and his family all of my junior year. Thankfully, I was able to share their meals. I worked hard for that dairy farmer. It took over two hours to pump water with an old rusty hand pump for more than forty head of cattle. After pumping water, the dairy farmer would milk at least twelve cows by hand and I would milk ten. Then we bottled the milk. After supper, we took the freshly bottled milk to Princeton. My employer would drive the truck. I ran to the houses to deliver the milk and pick up the empty bottles set out by our customers. I started my homework assignments when we returned home around ten o'clock at night. After a few hours of sleep, we would begin the morning chores at four o'clock. We milked the cows, bottled the milk, ate a quick breakfast, and delivered the milk. He dropped me off at school in time for my first period class. After school I ran four miles back to the farm and started the process again. The work was hard and time-consuming, but I was thankful for a warm place to sleep, food to eat and a little money for tuition. This job became my FFA project for my junior year, but I was too busy to attend many of the meetings, or hold an office in the FFA.

My beautiful sister, Vee and William Alley planned to be married the first week of November. Reva and I were the witnesses at their wedding. The small ceremony was held in their pastor's living room. Vee and my new brother-in-law, Bill planned a wonderful honeymoon to the World's Fair in Chicago, Illinois. Bill's parents paid for the trip as a wedding present. This brought back many memories for our dad, of the St. Louis World's fair he attended many years before.

During my junior year, I was too busy for sports or other activities, but I did one thing I will never forget. I attended the National FFA Convention and the American Royal, located in Kansas City, Missouri. My vocational agriculture teachers, Mr. Tumbelson and Mr. Arney, had explained the purpose and importance of these events during their classes. Both events were held annually and simultaneously in Kansas City. The American Royal Livestock show invited vocational agriculture students to participate in national livestock judging contests. I desperately wanted to go to those conventions. I had never been to Kansas City, or traveled any farther from home than Princeton, Missouri. I did not have transportation, money for food, admittance fees, or nice clothing needed for these events. However, I would not allow those minor details to keep me from attending. I convinced my friend, William Harris to go with me, and then told my employer I would be gone for a few days. Next I went to the Princeton stockyards and talked to a man who regularly purchased cattle and took them to Kansas City. He said we could ride with him. William and I were to meet him at the stockyards early the next morning. I went home and put a change of clothing and a few things in a pillowcase. I had less than a dollar in change. I was so excited I could hardly sleep that night.

The next morning was a chilly, November day. It looked like a storm was brewing. I met William at the stockyards about the time school was starting. We helped the truck driver load the cattle and waited for him in the cab of his truck. The trucker got in and told us to get out because he had another man riding with him. We reminded him that he said we could ride with him. He jerked his thumb toward the cattle and said, "Back there, boys." We were dumbfounded! There was nothing we could do but get out of the truck. He pulled a tarp over the truck that was very tightly loaded with cattle. He asked us to help him tie the tarp firmly over his load. William and I kept looking at each other, wondering what we were going to do.

When he got to the back of the truck, rather than tying off the tarp, he pointed to the space under the tarp and said, "Climb in boys." He showed us how to lie across the backs of the cows and hang onto the side rails of the truck. We hesitated only a moment before we got in. The truck driver finished tying the tarp over us and the cattle. William and I squirmed and wiggled, trying to get comfortable. Soon the truck took off amid the sounds of thunder and complaining cattle. William and I yelled to each other to hold on tight. The stench was stifling. The trucker stopped two times to check on us and let us get out to stretch. We were horribly uncomfortable, but I was thankful for two things; the tarp was keeping us from getting soaked and the cattle were so tightly packed they were nearly unable to move.

The first part of our trip was not going quite as smoothly as we had planned. Nevertheless, we were accomplishing our goal to get to Kansas City. After a very long trip we finally arrived at the huge Kansas City stockyards. I was amazed by the size of the place. There were open areas and areas under roof. There were sections for hogs, cattle, sheep and animals of all kinds. Trucks were arriving and departing, and people were hustling the livestock. We were seeing amazing sights in Kansas City. William and I helped the truck driver unload his cattle, thanked him, and began searching for someone to give us directions to the American Royal. We began walking with our pillowcases slung over our shoulders. Just walking the length of the stockyards was quite a distance. The rain had stopped and the temperatures were dropping. We walked and walked, asking people along the way for directions. Finally, we saw the American Royal. We entered what I assumed was a side door. We saw outstanding specimens of hogs, sheep and cattle. We tried to see what we could, even though it was closing for the day. We found stacks of hay bales located near the cattle stalls and slept there for the night.

The next morning we put on clean shirts and used water from the stock tank to wash up a little. I suspect we were quite a sight. We walked around the arenas with our sacks and tried to see everything going on. There were vendors giving tiny samples of food products. Those snacks were our meal for the day. We asked for directions to the National FFA Convention. I hoped it was nearby, but it was quite a distance away. As we walked toward downtown Kansas City, it became obvious, even to two country boys, this was a rough and unsafe part of the city. We witnessed things we had never even heard about. The area was densely populated, which was interesting and different from what we were accustomed to. We saw a soup kitchen with a long line of people waiting to be fed. We did not stop because we thought it was for poor people. It never occurred to me that I was poor.

We arrived at the large hall where the National FFA Convention was held. It was a very large building with several floors. The first floor had rows of exhibits. William and I looked at each one. They were filled with interesting projects, products and ideas from every area of the nation. Next, we went to a huge meeting room. We found seats very high up and watched part of the convention. We heard them discuss and vote on a specific jacket for FFA members. Blue corduroy jackets became the official FFA dress code.

William had relatives in Kansas City. He found a pay phone and spent a nickel to call them. They gave us directions to their house. It was a long way from the downtown area. We had to take a streetcar and then walk the rest of the way. They were a nice family with three small children. They were poor, but kindly allowed us to sleep on their floor that night. They did not have any blankets for us. The next morning they fed us a small meal and went to the FFA Convention with us. At the end of the day, William went home with his relatives. He planned to catch a ride to Princeton the following day with another family they knew. They did not have room for me. We parted ways and I continued on by myself.

That night I walked back to the American Royal through the same rough neighborhood. This time I was by myself. I sprinted part of the way to get there before dark. Once again, I slept on the hay bales near the livestock. Some other teenagers were sleeping there as well. They were FFA students showing their animals. No one asked me why I was there. I think everyone assumed I was one of the FFA students waiting to have my livestock judged. The next morning I walked back to the Kansas City Stockyards. I was able to find a truck driver heading north, after he unloaded his cattle to sell. He said he was going to Trenton, Missouri. It was late in the evening when we went through Cameron. About eight miles outside of Trenton, Missouri, he turned off on a small dirt road and stopped. I was surprised when he said this was as far as he was going.

Apparently he lived down this road. There was nothing I could do but get out of his truck and hope another vehicle would come by. It was so late the traffic had stopped. In the distance I saw cattle in a field and a small open shed. I thought perhaps I could sleep in the shed until daylight. As I started walking that direction a bull came toward me, snorting. Although weary and cold, I continued walking toward Trenton.

I saw a ditch on a side road with straw next to it and decided this would be a good bed for a few hours until daylight. When the sun came up, I caught a ride to the edge of Trenton. I imagine I was looking and smelling like the cattle I slept with by this time. Surely it was the favor of God that persuaded someone to give me a ride. I walked through Trenton to get to Highway 65, the road that led to Princeton. From there, I was able to hitch a ride to Princeton. I arrived home that night, milked cows, bottled the milk and made the deliveries with my employer. It was wonderful to have a hot meal and a bed to sleep in.

The following day at school, I was given a note to see my principal. He asked me where I had been the past few days. I told him about my adventure. I could tell he was amazed by my story. After asking questions to glean more details, he explained that due to unexcused absences, I would need to go to detention for one hour after school, for five days. This actually gave me a chance to catch up on my homework. Five hours of detention was worth every minute of my adventure. This trip from the country to a big city was the highlight of my school year.

Reva and I were able to finish our junior year in high school with good grades. We both matured and learned many life skills in school and on our jobs. Growing up in the Depression was a real life classroom, teaching us how to be innovative, frugal and self-sufficient.

That summer, Reva and I went home to the family farm to help our parents any way we could. But this was a very different kind of summer. It was over 100 degrees by the end of May. The entire summer was extremely hot. No one had air conditioning. We had little rain and experienced a record-breaking drought across the country. Temperatures were frequently over 100 degrees while we were working in the garden and fields. We were able to harvest very little of our crops and suffered an almost total loss. The corn literally burned up from the sun. It was a terrible year for farmers in our area and nationwide. My father said he could not remember a summer that had been as hot and dry as this one. This worsened the effects of the Depression and resulted in even lower cash income for the farmers. Sadly, more local farmers, including our friends and extended family, left their farms to find employment wherever they could. Some headed to California and the northwest to find work. Conditions were much worse in Texas, New Mexico and Oklahoma. It was so dry they began to have fires and dust storms.

Reva and I prepared for our senior year of high school. Darrell was ready for his freshman year at Princeton High School. We planned to help Darrell get a good start in high school, just as Vee had helped Reva and me. Vee and Bill had moved to her husband's family farm near Mercer, Missouri. Her in-laws, the Alley family, also owned a home in Princeton, where they now lived. My parents rented an upstairs room from them for Darrell and me that was very satisfactory. It even had heat for the winter months. Reva got a job with a family with children to care for, and lived with them. I was excited to get a job in a feed store. The hours were much better than the dairy farm work I had done the year before. I was blessed by not having to run four miles home after school each day. I worked at the feed store after school, and about three nights a week. The nighttime work consisted of going with the owner as he took a truckload of eggs from Princeton to Kirksville, Missouri. I was hired to load and unload the eggs. The distance was about 100 miles each way. We usually didn't get home until three in the morning. I attended school every day, regardless of how tired I felt. This job was my FFA project for the year, and provided the money needed for rent and tuition.

Darrell loved all of his high school courses. He was soon a top student in his class, and made the honor roll his first semester. Once again, G.K. Arney was the vocational agriculture instructor. I got Darrell involved in the FFA. He enjoyed it as much as I did, and it was fun to go with him.

Darrell was concerned about his growth because he was very small for his age. He was teased about his height. I wanted to defend him, but he was plucky and did not allow the teasing to discourage him. He took care of himself by using his sense of humor. He wrote letters to my parents explaining his concerns about his lack of growth. Mom and Dad sent him to a local doctor. The doctor did not think there was anything physically wrong, and encouraged Darrell by saying he would have a growth spurt soon. He remained somewhat small in stature, much like our mother, but in time he did get that growth spurt.

Unfortunately, the drought continued. The Depression was getting steadily worse, and farmers were not making enough to get by. In spite of this, God blessed Darrel and me with a little food that year. About once a month, Vee and Bill would bring us produce from their farm when they visited his parents, our landlords. The Alleys occasionally shared something Mrs. Alley had prepared. My parents made a trip to Princeton two times that year and brought home-canned food to us. They sold eggs at the feed store where I was employed, to pay for their trip to town. This was a tremendous blessing. It was much easier to keep our energy level up with a good meal every few days.

In April of 1935, a huge dust storm devastated much of Oklahoma and Texas. It was caused by the long drought and poor farm land management. Many people died covered in dirt. Every newspaper and radio station talked about it. It was discussed at great length in my vocational agriculture class. Because it occurred on a Sunday, and was so destructive, it was called Black Sunday. Three hundred thousand tons of topsoil was blown away. Uncle Will Hagan, Dad's next older brother, was living near Watonga, Oklahoma, on a farm he had homesteaded in 1907. Uncle Will and Aunt Kitty lived in the middle of what had been a wheat-producing area. In his letters to Dad, Uncle Will related that no matter how tightly he and Aunt Kitty sealed their home, they could not keep the dirt from entering the house. Their two sons lived nearby. They were unable to earn a living farming and no other jobs were available. The last time I had seen my handsome Uncle Will was at Granddad Hagan's funeral. Drought first hit the country in 1930 and by 1934, had turned the Great Plains into a desert.

1935 Princeton High School Graduates
Reva Pearle Hagan and Raymond Dale Hagan

Even though farmers in north Missouri and Iowa were struggling, they were doing well compared with the situation other farmers faced in the southern plains states, especially Oklahoma. Our family prayed for Uncle Will and Aunt Kitty to be safe and blessed with food and rain.

Our senior class was the first class at Princeton High School with a large number of country students. We were also the largest graduating class at Princeton High School, with sixty-three seniors walking at commencement. Because country students were not well received by the town students, many did not complete high school. They could not tolerate the harassment. Against all odds, Reva and I graduated in May of 1935. We were thin, but thankful we had survived the past four years. I think these experiences made us better people, unafraid to confront our futures, regardless of circumstances we might face.

Being an optimist – no matter what!

My brother Albert also graduated from the University of Missouri in May of 1935. The entire family was very proud of Albert. He graduated at the top of his class, with a degree in agriculture. He was the first college graduate in our family. My handsome oldest brother was an inspiration to all of his younger siblings.

Reva and Darrell returned to the farm as soon as the school year ended, but I continued working at the feed store for a few weeks after graduation. I was only making enough money to buy a hamburger once a day and pay my room rent. I had a dream to go to college to be an extension agent. Missouri University was the only school in the state offering a degree in agriculture. Sadly, I had no money to fund my dream.

Raymond Hagan in 1935

I made appointments with two well-respected high school teachers, to ask their advice about attending college. They both told me the same thing. Due to the Depression it would be impossible to go to college unless someone furnished the money. Because there were no jobs in Columbia, Missouri, many college students dropped out of school. Disappointed, I told my teachers I had no money. No one I knew had any money. Attending college seemed unattainable for me. Working for rent and a daily hamburger was a dead-end road. Farm life was something I would enjoy, but due to the unavailability of farm loans and the current market prices for livestock and crops, farming also appeared to be an impossible dream for me. That evening I prayed for guidance about what to do with my life. I asked the Lord to guide me in everything I did. Late that night, I made the only decision that gave me a strong sense of peace.

Chapter 14

THE IMPOSSIBLE DREAM

The next day after work, I went to the bank in Princeton and asked to see the banker. Mr. Coon asked me what I wanted. I explained I was going to the University of Missouri to begin college. He asked me how I would get there. I told him I would hitchhike. Next, he asked where I would stay. My reply was honest. I had no idea. He inquired how much money I wanted to borrow. I said "Fifteen dollars." He looked at me and repeated, "Fifteen dollars?" with sarcasm in his voice. I could tell that he was fighting back a chuckle. After a moment of deliberation, Mr. Coon handed me the money and prepared a loan document for my signature.

That night I called my parents to tell them my decision. The next day they came to Princeton to say good-bye and bought me a dollar suitcase. They were broke just like everyone else in the Depression, and had no money to give me. Dad told me that he and Raycel were having trouble getting the crops planted, because the weather had been unusually cold and wet. I was thankful for the lavish gift because I knew their financial situation was desperate. No matter what I wanted to do with my life, I was grateful my parents were loving and supportive. I knew they were going to pray for me every day.

I had very little to put in my new suitcase. Everything I owned easily fit inside, with room to spare. The next evening I caught a ride in the produce truck going to Kirksville, Missouri. I helped unload the eggs in the rain and said goodbye to my employer. I slept on the floor of the warehouse without a blanket. The floor was hard and so cold, I was shaking.

When the sun came up, I walked to Highway 63. I had looked at a map and thought it would be about one mile, but it was five miles away. Once I got to the highway, I stuck out my thumb to people passing by. This was a signal hitchhikers used to indicate they needed a ride. In the Depression years, hitchhikers

The impossible dream

were a common sight. I finally caught a ride with a trucker and explained I was traveling to Columbia to attend college. He kept talking about St. Louis, so I thought when he got to Highway 40 he would turn east toward St. Louis. When I saw a Highway 40 sign, I said I wanted out there. He gave me an odd look, but didn't say anything. He stopped to let me out. I was surprised when he drove straight across the highway toward Columbia. I had assumed he would turn toward St Louis since he was talking about it. Obviously, I never thought to ask and he was too polite to question why I would get out before we got to Columbia. Carrying my new suitcase, I walked the last six miles to Columbia.

I didn't know where I was going to stay, but remembered my older brother Albert saying he stayed at the Farmhouse. I didn't know it was a fraternity. I assumed it was a home for farm boys. I finally found the Farmhouse and rang the doorbell. A young man answered the door and said, "What do you want?" I said, "I am looking for a place to stay." He said, "The house is closed for the summer. A few of us are staying here to look after it." He shut the door and I started to leave. The door opened and another young man looked out and asked, "What is your name?" I said, "Ray Hagan." He asked, "Do you know Al Hagan?" I said, "Yes, he is my brother." He said "I know Al. We went to the state college together in Maryville. Come in, you can stay with me." Albert was a member of that fraternity. I lived at the Farmhouse that summer and the fall of my freshman year.

The next several days I walked all over Columbia looking for a job. It helped me to become familiar with this big city. One day I went into the large Dixie Café on Eighth Street in downtown Columbia. I bought a hamburger because it was the least expensive item on the menu. While I was waiting for my daily meal, I asked the owner if he needed help. He said no, but wrote my name in a spiral notebook and mumbled maybe some time he would need help. I assumed the notebook was full of names of people looking for a job. I continued to eat there every day, having a hamburger and water, since that was all I could afford. A few weeks later, I asked the same gentleman, "Would you mind if I worked here for experience?" He said, "Experience?" I said, "Everywhere I have applied for a job, they want to know if I have any experience." He sat there for a moment, and then called out to Lucy, a young waitress, "Get this young man an apron and show him how to wait tables." After that, I waited tables for lunch and supper. After a week, he asked, "Do you want a job for your meals?" Excitedly I said, "I sure do!" He indicated I would have to work at night. I replied that would be fine. He said the hours would be from nine o'clock until one-thirty in the morning, serving college students. I said that would be great. He said I would have to serve beer along with the food. I immediately thought about Mom and what she taught me in Sunday school. Finally, I said that I would. I worked at the Dixie Café for a year and a half.

I now had a place to stay and a way to get two meals a day. With this accomplished, I began looking for another job. I literally applied at every place I could find. One morning I went to the university library and asked to see the person in charge. I was ushered into a man's office. He seemed very busy. I told him I needed a job. He gave a little speech about the economy. The university only gave him enough money to hire four students for the summer to work the circulation desk. He planned to give each employee $30 a month. I left, but could not stop thinking about the library. After praying that evening, I decided to visit him again. I explained to him that I had pondered what he told me. It occurred to me that instead of hiring four students and paying them thirty dollars a month, he could hire eight students and pay them fifteen dollars a month. He was quite surprised and insisted that no one could live on fifteen dollars a month. I said that I could. After a little more discussion, he said to come back the following day. He gave me a job for thirty dollars a month, but explained that I would have to enroll in summer school. I said I would enroll. He nearly burst my bubble when he said I needed to enroll by the deadline, which was the very next day. He directed me to the business offices at Jesse Hall.

I went to a large building with a sign that read Jesse Hall. It was an involved process to enroll at Missouri University for the first time. With a lot of help, I completed the admissions papers. I was sent down the hall to the payment window to finish my enrollment. I went to that little window and turned in the paperwork. A woman carefully looked it over and said it was all in order and I needed to pay the tuition. I said, "I don't have that much money." In a stern voice she said very loudly, "I can't enroll you if you don't pay!" I explained to her I would get the money, but I did not have it now. We went over this several times and people were beginning to stare at us. She became frustrated and sent me to see her supervisor. I was more than a little nervous as I went through the door to talk to her. I had the identical conversation with her. I quietly asked God to help me. She kept insisting she could not enroll me without money. I kept promising her I would have it after I started working. I could not start working unless I was enrolled. Finally she said, "We have never done this before, but I will enroll you." She shook her finger in my face and said sternly, "If you don't pay before the summer is over, you will get an F." I was enrolled in the University of Missouri. This was step one on the road to be an extension agent. God had shown me favor, when everyone said it was an impossible dream.

My class schedule worked out very well. I had class for one period, and then worked at the library for the next two periods. The Lord provided me with a place to stay, a job for my meals, a job for my tuition and, best of all, I was enrolled in summer school. The thing I didn't have was money. So I started looking for another job. I looked everywhere for a job and met a variety of people around Columbia.

One day I saw an ad for a sheep grading day at the fairgrounds. I walked to the fairgrounds and located a gentleman who seemed to be in charge. I asked if he needed help. He informed me they needed a lot of help, but didn't have money to pay anybody. I told him, "Since I am not busy, I'll help anyway." I found out he was the county extension agent. I enjoyed working with the sheep. I was accustomed to handling them on Dad's farm.

I firmly believe there are no coincidences in life. A few days later, I was working at the Dixie Café when the County Agent, who ran the sheep grading contest at the fairgrounds, brought in a gentleman to eat lunch. He introduced me to his friend. His friend was a landscaper in Columbia. He was driving a truck with a variety of equipment in the back. I was aware of the men talking about me. While serving them lunch, I talked with the landscaper, and mentioned I needed a job. He had seven men working for him taking care of trees, lawns and shrubs at houses and businesses around Columbia. He invited me to ride with him to see what he was doing. I was excited. I rode around town with him the next few days. He would have one or two men working at each job site. He dropped them off with the necessary equipment and explained their assignments. Later he would return to check their progress and drive them to the next job location. Then he went to another work site where he had another team of men working and explained what their jobs involved. He had men working at three different places. He kept detailed records of the work each man completed. After I rode around with him a few days he said, "If you will keep my record books up-to-date and help me show them what to do, I will give you a job." Without hesitation, I took the job I never thought to ask how much he would pay me.

Everything went well that summer. I attended class, had a place to stay, a way to get meals, and was making a little money. God provided a way for me to attend college. I believe this was possible because I had followed His direction, after praying that night in Princeton.

Darrell wrote humorous letters, keeping me up-to-date on the farm and our family. He told me that my sweet cousin, Wilma had married Ronald Vaughn, and that her mother, Aunt Grace was having continuous lung issues. Uncle Ernest was very concerned about her. Darrell said Dad had been able to sell a yearling and two other head of cattle for a total of $190. This was cause for celebration and the money was used to pay on the farm mortgage and taxes. I felt a wave of homesickness while reading his letters. I still have these letters preserved as cherished keepsakes.

When summer school was almost over, the landscaper mentioned he was going on vacation for two months. I was surprised when he said he wanted me to keep his business going while he was gone. I asked him how I would know what to do. His said he would show me during the next few days. While he explained my duties, I asked how I was going to get the workers to the job sites. He planned to leave his truck for me to drive. Now that was a problem. I had only driven one time when I lived at Granddad Hagan's farm. I was honest and told him I had no idea how to drive the landscaping truck. He considered that a few minutes and said he was willing to teach me how to drive. During the next few days, I was the driver as we kept the business going. He was a patient man. Missouri did not require a driver's license at that time. In the back of my mind, I remembered reading in one of Darrell's letters that Reva had wrecked Raycel's car in front of the house while learning to drive. I was hoping I did not have a similar issue in the landscaping truck.

Finally, my employer and driving instructor told me he would be leaving on vacation the next day. He planned to take a train to Canada, and wanted me to drop him off at the train depot, and then keep his truck to use for work. Apparently, he trusted me. The timing worked out very well for me, as summer term had ended and the library would be closed between semesters.

Everything went smoothly for several days. Early one morning, I left three men at one work site, gave them instructions and explained that I would be back at ten o'clock. When I returned, they had done very little and two of them were sitting under a shade tree. I explained they needed to get the job done. They were grown men. I probably looked like a skinny kid to them, yet I was telling them what to do. One of them got up and started to work, but another one said, "It's too hot and I am not going to." I informed him that was fine and he could go home. He sarcastically said, "You can't fire me." The other man said, "Yes he can. I heard the boss tell Ray, 'If the workers don't cooperate you should tell them to go home.'" He sat there a short time, then got up and left. I was relieved he did not try to hit me with the shovel.

Following this episode, I never had another worker refuse to do what I told them to do. When my employer returned from his trip, he carefully looked over the records and inspected each work site, and told me everything was more than acceptable. Best of all, in my mind, the truck had not been wrecked. We never discussed the salary he planned to pay me. I was amazed when he gave me enough money to pay for both fall and winter tuition, and pay off my $15 loan at the bank in Princeton. I was elated. I kept thanking God for His timely provision. I told my employer my hours would change when the fall semester started. I would attend class, and continue working at both the library and the restaurant. I would be able to help him only on Saturday and Sunday. He agreed to those hours because it would give him the weekends off work.

My little sister, Reva married Charlie Cornett in September of 1935. Charlie grew up nearby, in Iowa. Reva and I had always been very close and frequently wrote letters to each other. I was happy for Reva, but sad that I could not attend her wedding. It made me realize that marriage could not be in my future for several years, if I wanted to continue my education.

A few weeks later, in the fall of 1935, the owner of the Dixie Café said he would be gone the next weekend. There was an important university football game and he expected an extremely large lunch crowd before the game. He planned to add as many long, lunch tables as possible in the large back room. He wanted me to help his sister serve the customers. Her husband would run the cash register, and two other waitresses would work the front room. That Saturday I went to the restaurant early to help his sister prepare the back room for the expected crowd. She wanted me to help their regular waitress in the larger back room and she and another temporary waitress would take care of the front room. They heard a large group of people from Kansas City and St. Louis were coming for the football game and planned to have lunch at the cafe.

As if on cue, at eleven-thirty, people started pouring into the cafe. I seated them and gave them lunch menus. It became so crowded that people were sharing chairs. I saw the regular waitress standing at the entrance of the back room. She looked very distressed, raised her arms and said, "I'm not doing this." She turned and ran out the front door.

Now I was alone in that crowded back room. I didn't know what to do, so I raised my hands into the air and talked loudly to get everyone's attention. I said, "Our regular waitress is not here. I am new at this, but I will try to serve you. If you want to go somewhere else I will understand." A few customers left, but most stayed. I continued to take customers' orders to the kitchen and served drinks as fast as possible. The kitchen workers let me know when they had orders ready to serve. I brought out all the meals I could carry on large trays and set them on the table. I tried to serve the correct meal to each customer, but I had trouble identifying the food. One customer jumped up and started helping me. He could serve the food as fast as I could carry it out. Finally, I had served everyone and they hurried off to the game. Suddenly the back room was empty. As I began cleaning the tables, I discovered many of the customers rushed away and left their money on the tables. I found several five and ten dollar bills, many one dollar bills and handfuls of change. It was more cash than I had ever seen at one time. After I finished cleaning the room, I took the money and gave it to the man at the cash register. I told him the customers had forgotten their money. He smiled at me and indicated they would probably come back after the money, so he would keep it for them. A few weeks later I learned it was called tip money. Tipping was something I had never heard of. I did not realize the tips were for me. I decided to ask the man at the cash register about it. He said they didn't come after it, so he put it in the cash register drawer. I didn't believe him, but there was nothing I could do about it.

My freshman year was busy with three jobs and school, but I was diligent about class attendance. No matter how tired I felt, I never cut a class. The instructors kept daily attendance records. These college classes required more work than my high school classes. There were more papers to write and a great deal of reading.

The Farmhouse fraternity required so many obligations, I decided to move out the following spring. I rented a tiny apartment with another young man, who also left the Farmhouse. We split the cost of the rent. His parents sent him money for school, so he did not need to work. He had grown up close to Princeton in Chillicothe, Missouri.

I finished my freshman year at Missouri University in the spring of 1936. During this time, our country was in a drought lasting longer than any in recorded history. It resulted in what was called a "dust bowl" in the Midwest. We had little rain that spring. The trees, shrubs, and grass turned brown. Because the ground was dry, when the wind blew the air was full of dust. Dust and dirt literally blew in our faces and swirled into dust storms. We were told that Oklahoma and Kansas were in even worse condition than Missouri.

I debated what to do the summer following my freshman year. Our country was in a huge financial mess, in spite of the now famous "New Deal" our president implemented. I was very homesick at times and considered going back to the farm for the summer. It was pleasant to think about Mother's cooking, the fun I would have working with my brothers and seeing my friends and cousins. I could be of assistance to my parents and Raycel on the farm. After careful consideration, I realized if I left my jobs, I would likely not have them in the fall. I enrolled in summer school and kept working all three jobs.

Never had I experienced such incredibly hot days. Extreme heat resulted in setting new records across the country. The summer heat was so intolerable that many families slept outside to escape the heat of their houses. I worked outside for the landscaping company and went home at night to an upstairs room that felt like a furnace. No one had air conditioning. The university library was stifling, but thankfully it did have ceiling fans.

In one of my classes, the professor told us that soil temperatures in Oklahoma reached two hundred degrees just below the surface. That was as hot as an oven. Farmers experienced crop failure nationwide, causing corn and wheat prices to rise quickly. I still kept the chart on the markets that I started as

The impossible dream

a freshman in high school, in Mr. Tumbleson's agriculture classes. Things did not look good for our country.

The Dust Bowl affected more than Oklahoma, Kansas, Texas, New Mexico and Colorado, where it started. The unanchored soil turned to dust and blew away in clouds that turned the sky black. These were called "black blizzards" or "black rollers." These dust storms reached Columbia, Missouri, and went all the way to New York City and Washington, D.C. We covered our faces with handkerchiefs, but still choked on the dust. In just minutes, the horrible dust was in our eyes, hair, shoes and mouths. On bad days it would get in our food and on the clean dishes. The landscaping business also suffered as the hot sun burned up everything. Some of our workers had heat strokes and became sick from the oppressive heat.

Walking about Columbia on my way to class and work, I noticed that housewives used their dishwater to water tomato plants and wash the dust off of porches. This was a way to conserve water. As the summer went on, the dust kept getting worse and was blowing around constantly.

One day I was walking to the south edge of the agriculture campus on my way to class, suddenly a strong wind kicked up dust so thick I could hardly see. I met no one else walking. When I finally made it to the livestock building, where my class was held, I saw a fire in the pasture below the building. I went inside the building and found it was empty. I noticed a large bucket full of water and decided I would try to stop the fire from reaching the campus. When I walked onto the field, it was covered with crunchy, dead bluegrass. The air was so full of smoke and dust I could hardly see. My eyes watered and I choked from breathing the smoke-filled air. Every few minutes a strong wind gust caused the fire to spread. A woven wire fence ran away from campus down the hill. On the other side of the fence was a crop of tall dead hay. I knew if the wildfire got to the hay it would be unstoppable. I found a gunny sack to dip in the water and used it to keep the fire from spreading. I worked for what seemed like an hour or two keeping the fire away from the fence.

Finally, I saw a large fire truck and fire fighters running everywhere. One of them came to me and yelled, "What are you are doing?" I said as loudly as my dry mouth allowed, "Keeping the fire off that hay field." He explained they would handle it. I walked back to the livestock building. I was covered with smoke and ashes and dust had filled my shoes, pockets and ears. As I walked into the building, I ran into the professor who taught the class I was taking. He had a shocked look on his face when he asked, "What in the world are you doing outside?" I told him what I had been doing. He asked if I heard the announcement on the radio that said the campus was closed because of the strong wind and dust. I told him I was unaware of the warning, as I didn't own a radio. One good result of this incident was that the professor became my trusted lifelong friend.

I began my sophomore year at the university in the fall of 1936. The dusty wind was still a problem. I was busy day and night, going to school, working at the library and the restaurant. Some of my classes were so difficult and time-consuming that I cut my class load down to fifteen hours.

One of the highlights of the fall of 1936 was good news from my little sister, Reva and her husband, Charlie. They had a baby girl named Melva Ann. I wanted to go to Pleasanton, Iowa to visit them. Sometimes waves of homesickness would overtake me as I thought of my family and the beautiful farm in North Missouri, but I persevered as I could not risk losing the jobs I had struggled so hard to find. Being frugal was a necessity, but I did go to a movie twice with friends. It cost ten cents to see a movie. That was the same price as a hamburger, so once in a while I would skip lunch to see a movie.

This was a presidential election year. Our country was still in the throes of the Great Depression and weather atrocities like those dust storms were making economic recovery nearly impossible. I thought we should not change national leadership in the midst of crisis. For the first time, at the age of twenty-one, I voted in the elections. President Roosevelt, better known as FDR, and his party won a landslide victory in early November.

One of my friends told me about an intramural wrestling competition. It sounded like fun, because I had loved wrestling with my brothers growing up. I signed up to enter the tournament. I pinned the first three opponents in my weight class. The fourth man won the match on points because he ran from me. I did not have a clue how to stop him. The wrestling coach seemed impressed and asked me to join the wrestling team. I practiced with students in my weight class and in other weight classes. I was never pinned, but did lose some matches on points. When the team was preparing to go to a wrestling tournament in Nebraska, the coach scheduled an elimination match to determine which wrestler to take in each weight class. He matched me with the captain of the team. Amazingly, I won the match. That young man was good enough to get up off the mat, shake my hand, congratulate me and tell me I could go on the trip to Nebraska. I was very excited to be part of the team, and to go to another state, other than Iowa, for the first time in my life.

Chapter 15

THE DAY I DIED

Unfortunately, I was unable to go on the trip to Nebraska. That fall, an influenza epidemic spread throughout the nation and many hospitals were full of patients. Perhaps the influenza was caused in part by the dust we were breathing. The influenza sometimes developed into a disease called Dust Pneumonia.

Many university students were sick and many died. I had not felt well since the elimination match. One afternoon, while working at the library, I became very sick and so weak I could not walk up and down the stairway. The director of the library sent me to the university hospital to be checked out. A doctor examined and admitted me to the hospital for observation. The rooms and hallways were full of patients on cots. The next morning, when the doctor was making rounds, I put on my clothes and sat waiting for him on the edge of my cot. When he asked how I was feeling, I told him I was fine and was able to leave. He had the nurse discharge me. I know he released me because they needed the bed. All local hospitals were at capacity, so Reed Hall, a large three-story brick building, was turned into an emergency hospital.

I went back to work and class. In two days, I felt so sick I could hardly walk straight. My supervisor at the library sent me back to the hospital. The doctor took one look at me and told the nurse to put me in a bed right away. Instead of putting me on a cot, she took me to a little closet they had cleaned out and made into a private room. I had a bad earache. The doctor came in, looked in my ear and said he would have to lance it. A large nurse held my head while the doctor lanced my eardrum. It was the most excruciating pain I had ever felt in my life. He turned me over to the side he had lanced and told me to keep that ear down so it could drain. I was placed in a room with other students. All of us were coughing relentlessly. I was diagnosed with the flu and later developed pneumonia. My skin was burning, but I felt very cold.

Later that night, the nurse came in to check on me. I told her I felt better, but didn't think my ear had been draining. She told me if my ear did not drain they would have to lance it again. I said I would climb out the window before I let that happen again! I tried to sound strong, but actually I was weak as a kitten. The next day, I was not aware of what was going on around me because I slept most of the time. I had a high temperature and heaviness in my chest.

I sensed myself getting weaker and sicker. I felt terrible and had a tremendous headache. My chest hurt and I was cold to my bones. When the nurses came to check on me, I could no longer tell them how I was doing.

Suddenly, I felt like I was floating through the air. My body was not hurting or struggling to breathe. What a relief! I looked down and could see myself lying on the cot in the hospital room. There were two nurses working on me. I saw the entire hospital, every floor and every room. Some of the patients were students I knew. The walls didn't hinder me. I could see everything. I could see three floors down into the hospital basement. There was a large room filled with equipment for preparing food, refrigerators, counters, pans and cooking stoves, much like a cafeteria. Everything was clean and the utensils were neatly organized. It seemed to be closed because no one was working there or preparing food.

I watched as the two nurses continued working over me. One nurse was short and the other one was thin and extremely tall. The tall nurse had her hair pulled up in a bun, with two stick-like holders keeping her nurse's cap on and her hair up. She had a very ornate hairstyle. I could see every detail. Ordinarily, this would have been impossible for me, because she was at least a foot taller than me.

Then I rose up and out of the hospital. I saw my parents' farm in North Missouri, even though in reality it was hours away. I saw it plainly as though I was up very high, looking down on it. I saw hundreds of acres; the farm, the house, the barn, and everything around it. I could see the livestock and horses. It is difficult to describe what else I saw and felt in this place I will call the spirit world. It is difficult to describe the spirit world because we do not have words in our language that clearly convey what is reality in that world. Our words only explain what is known on earth.

I can compare being in the spirit world to a fish bowl where many fish are swimming together, aware of other fish near them, but not touching each other. Just like those fish, I felt there were many people around me. I was moving around and they were too. I recognized some of them as family members who had died before me. We were aware of each other, could communicate, and knew what was going on around us and on Earth. We were enveloped by the Spirit of God. We were comfortable and happy and one in the Spirit of the Lord. I was enveloped in his spirit of love.

I felt wonderful and no longer had pain. I experienced a freedom I never knew existed. I could go anywhere, instantly. Walls were not a barrier. I could see and move through them. Distance was no longer a consideration. I simply went places instantly by thinking about them. I could communicate without talking. I only needed to think it to be understood. This made communication easy and without misunderstandings. I experienced various emotions while in that state. My strongest feeling was all-consuming peace and comfort, both physically and emotionally. I was entirely accepted, loved and safe. My body was no longer freezing cold. The temperature was perfect! I was happy and very contented there. All my earthly problems were gone. Time was not important in this place. What took hours on Earth seemed to take only moments now.

I continued to watch as the nurses worked over my physical body. They pulled the sheet up and over my head. They did something with my feet. Later, I learned they were putting a toe tag on me. They spoke about getting a doctor to sign my death certificate.

Later, my family and friends explained that I was reported dead. My name was given on the radio news as one of the University of Missouri students who had died in the flu epidemic. When my parents were notified of my death they began the long trip to Columbia to bring my body home.

The next thing I saw was amazing. It seemed as though I was looking at a large mural, or a movie. In what seemed like an instant, I saw my whole life in front of me. I saw it all, every bit of it; every incident and every detail. It was colorful and every detail precise. I saw the people I had known throughout my life; family, teachers and friends. In this place, if I thought about the family farm, in an instant I was there. I saw every day, week, month, and year, in what seemed like a few brief minutes. Everything I had done during my lifetime was visible. My thoughts were simply, "I haven't done much yet. I want to go back and live!" I felt no pain, enjoyed new freedom of movement, delighted in the love of God, but still, I wanted to go back. There were many things I wanted to do in my life.

My thoughts were the way I communicated with the Lord. There was no need to speak. The Lord heard everything I communicated and responded according to my thoughts. The Lord kindly agreed that I could return to my body.

After more than twenty-four hours in this beautiful spirit world, I re-entered my body. Again, I knew I was very sick. I had all the discomforts I had felt before I left my body. I was now in a storeroom filled with equipment. No other living people were around me. This room had been set up as a temporary morgue, until the bodies of those who had died could be claimed by their families, or taken to a funeral home. This was necessary because the funeral homes were overflowing with victims of the epidemic. The next thing I remember were nurses trying to get me to breathe and forcing water down my throat.

My parents arrived at the hospital to take my body home. I found out how shocked and thankful they were when they were told I had returned from death. They had prayed for me all the way to Columbia. God had answered their prayers!

Some time after I returned to my body, my brother, Albert came to see me. I was still too weak to talk, but could hear and see everything. I was aware he was there with me. He brought me a radio and tuned it to a Kansas City radio station for me to listen to, as I recuperated. On the news report that night, I heard about the terrible flu epidemic at the University of Missouri. The radio reported the number of students who had died, and listed three students who had died in the last few days. I was one of the three. I knew one of the others very well. He was in my fraternity, the Farmhouse. I listened to the radio, but couldn't say anything or move because I was still very ill.

My family was contacted for assistance during this time. The medical staff told my family I needed a blood transfusion. The donated blood must match my blood type. Fortunately, my brother Albert was a match. He volunteered to do whatever he could to help me. The doctors and nurses set up a person-to-person blood transfusion, from Albert's arm to my arm. This was an unusual procedure done in desperation. This was apparently what my body needed. This loving and unselfish act of my big brother saved my life.

Slowly, I improved physically, and several days later began to talk. When the nurse came in, I asked her if they thought I was dead. She said, "Oh my!" as I told her what I saw and heard. She told me to wait a minute, and went to get the other nurse who had been caring for me. They both asked me questions. I told them everything I had seen, and heard them say. They stood there with their mouths and eyes wide open. They were shocked by what I told them. They quietly backed out of my room and said they would not bother me anymore.

About a week or two later, I was feeling well enough to get out of bed and sit in a chair. I woke up at 2:00 a.m. feeling extremely hungry. I rang the bell to tell the nurse I needed something to eat. She informed me that breakfast would not be served until 5:30 or 6:00 a.m. and not to worry, they would bring me food then. She left the room. I laid there a bit and thought, "But I need to eat something right now!" I got up and walked slowly down three flights of stairs to the basement and into the kitchen. I knew where I was going because I had seen the kitchen when I was moving freely in the spiritual realm. I had no idea there was a kitchen in the basement prior to that time. I went directly to the refrigerators and searched until I found something to eat. I ate until I felt better. With great effort, I slipped quietly upstairs to my bed. I continued to

Raymond Hagan
starting to recouperate from influenza

INFLUENZA CASES STILL INCREASING

Present Epidemic Not So Bad as Last Year's, Says Dr. Stine

The number of student patients at the University hospitals has increased to 128, Dr. Dan G. Stine, chairman of the University Health Service, reported this morning. This increase, along with the increase of the general hospital population, brought the total to 159, or a record high for this year.

Twenty-five patients were admitted during the twenty-four hours ending at 7 o'clock this morning, and eleven were discharged. The number of patients admitted exceeds that of a comparable period for last year's siege. However, Dr. Stine said, "On the whole, the present epidemic does not approach last year's in seriousness."

Raymond Hagan, College of Agriculture student who has been critically ill with pneumonia, is "much better," according to Dr. Stine, who said that Hagan showed further improvement after receiving a second blood transfusion.

Only three girls have been hospitalized at Read Hall, and Dr. Stine declares that the University Health Service is ready to meet any emergency.

Although the more recent cases admitted are more serious, Dr. Stine says that Hagan is the only patient within the danger zone.

It was reported that forty-seven students from the American government class, or approximately one-sixth of the enrollment, were absent today. This, and reports from other large classes which reveal an unusual number of absences, when compared to the smaller number of patients admitted to the hospitals, indicates that many students are remaining at home and away from crowds in order to protect themselves from influenza.

RAYMOND HAGAN ILL

Raymond Hagan, a student of the University of Missouri at Columbia, is ill with pneumonia fever, following an attack of influenza. He is confined to the University Hospital and is reported to be in a critical condition. He is a son of Mr. and Mrs. Ross Hagan of near Mercer.

gain strength as the days went by. One day the doctors felt I was well enough and released me to go home. I was still very weak. It took months before I felt somewhat normal and energetic again.

Shortly after I was dismissed from the hospital, I returned to work at the library. I knew the books that were available and located the ones containing writings about other people who had died and then came back to life. I read many of those stories. My experience is not just a story. It is true. I left my body behind, but my mind, thoughts and spirit kept on living. I was in the spirit world with the Lord and saw everything happening here on Earth. Many of the stories I read about other people's experiences were different than the way it had happened for me. Some related that after death, they went through a tunnel of fire. They were terrified and tormented. I did not go through a tunnel of fire. Perhaps, they went to hell. Although my experience was different than some of the stories I read, one thing remained the same. We all experienced a spiritual world and went there immediately after dying. We continued to live, but in a different kind of place and in a different way. The spirit world had been a wonderful experience for me, but a frightening one for others.

The difference between me and those going to a place of fire and pain became obvious to me. I thought back to a time in my childhood when I lived with my parents in North Missouri. I attended Bethel Church, where I learned about the Bible, the existence of the Lord and an after-life consisting of heaven and hell. To a young boy, heaven and hell seemed almost like a fairy tale, a place very far away. I was certainly more interested in riding horses, pitching a baseball and hunting than in thinking about life after death. I asked Jesus to be the Lord of my life during a two-week revival.

Making Jesus Lord of my life was the reason I went to a wonderful and beautiful place with the Lord when I died. Those going to a place of burning torment did not know the Lord. I am not afraid to die again one day. I know a wonderful experience is waiting for me. My spirit will remain there for all eternity and I will again feel comfort, peace and love surrounding me. Death for a Christian is not so much an exit out of life, as it is an entry into the Lord's presence.

2 Corinthians 5:8
"Yes, we are fully confident, and we would rather be away from these earthly bodies, for then we will be at home with the Lord." (NLT)

If you would like to know your future in the spirit world will be full of joy and happiness, you need to choose to be a follower of Jesus. It is simple and easy. This is a decision you must make now, while you are on earth. After your body dies, it is too late to choose. We are allowed a few years on Earth to consider our options and make the choice that determines where we will spend eternity. The Lord allows us to choose or reject Him. Here are the simple steps to take if you choose to be with Him forever. Say this simple prayer and mean it from you heart.

Dear God,
I admit I am a sinner and I need you in my life. Please forgive me of my sins. I believe Jesus died and rose again for my sins. I confess Jesus Christ is Lord and Savior of my life. Thank You for saving me and giving me abundant life here on earth and eternal life with You in heaven.
In Jesus' name, Amen.

<u>Your required actions–believe and confess.</u>

Romans 10:9-10
"That if you confess with your mouth, Jesus is Lord, and believe in your heart that God raised him from the dead, YOU WILL BE SAVED. For it is with your heart that you believe and are justified, and it is with your mouth that you confess and are saved."

<u>Your result is salvation – You are saved from an eternity in hell.</u>
<u>You will go to heaven when you die.</u>

Romans 10:13
"Everyone who calls on the name of the Lord WILL BE SAVED."

Acts 4:12
"Salvation is found in no one else, for there is no other name under heaven given to men by which we must be saved."

The spiritual world will be your home forever. Heaven or hell, you get to choose. You see, my friend, making no decision is a decision. It means you have decided not to go to heaven. If you prayed this little prayer, I will see you in heaven one day! What a blessing that will be!

Chapter 16

LIFE AFTER MY DEATH

Missing classes for six weeks meant I was not around to take finals at the semester's end. As soon as I was able to walk a little, I went to see my four professors. Three of them agreed to let me take the finals late, which allowed me to complete all the courses, except one. The final I was not allowed to take was for a five-hour math course. I tried several times to explain I had been in the hospital and there was no way I could have been in my seat for the final. He was unsympathetic and gave me an F for the course. I was frustrated because I had never had an F on my record. I was thankful I was able to study and pass the other three finals. The only one I was concerned about was agricultural engineering, because it was a difficult course and I had missed a great deal of lecture time. The professor gave me a helpful study guide, so I was able to earn an "S." I ended the semester with three "S's" and one "F." The next semester had already started. After another week, I discovered I was still not strong enough to walk across the university campus. I realized there was no way I could work or attend classes in my weakened condition.

After I completed the finals, I stayed with Reva and Charlie in Columbia, briefly, until I was strong enough to travel. I packed all my belongings in my suitcase and started hitchhiking home. I was still very weak. When I got to Moberly, I was so exhausted I could barely stand up. I saw a bus coming, so I flagged it down. The driver stopped and let me get in. I explained why I was hitchhiking. He said he was on the way to Kirksville, but allowed me to ride free to Macon. From there I was able to get a ride to Chillicothe and then caught another ride to Princeton. When I got to Princeton, I called my brother, Raycel to come get me. I was so exhausted, I needed his help lifting my suitcase into his car. My doctor advised me to stay out of school the spring semester. I remained weak for an extended period of time. By the end of six months, the fresh air and sunshine at the farm, along with Mom's wholesome cooking, helped me gain strength and a little weight.

While I was home, we heard from Uncle Will and Aunt Kitty Hagan in Oklahoma. After thirty years of hard work, they had lost their farm due to the extended drought and the horrible dust bowl. They were discouraged and unsure what to do. The dust had seriously affected Uncle Will's health. They decided with their two sons, Olin and Fred, to move to Tucson, Arizona. We prayed for them to find work and be successful. The "dirty thirties" were adversely affecting many people in our family.

Although I still felt exhausted, I decided to return to Columbia for summer school. I took an overload of hours to make up the classes I missed in the spring. The library director wanted me to increase the hours I worked there, so I was able to quit my job at the Dixie Café. This allowed me to get the additional rest I greatly needed. Although not at full strength physically, I was able to successfully complete my classes by summer's end. That meant I was on target to graduate with my class at the end of four years.

My major was Agricultural Economics because Mr. Tumbleson, my high school vocational agriculture teacher, was so enthusiastic about the subject. He convinced me this was an excellent choice. I took a few classes in Agricultural Economics, but did not like them very well. The classes seemed repetitious of my high school coursework.

I went to see my advisor at the beginning of my junior year. He asked how I was going to major in Agricultural Economics without taking the courses. That was a good question. He inquired if I was interested in something else, and suggested Agriculture Extension. He sent me to talk to the man in charge of Agriculture Extension. I enrolled in one semester of classes relating to extension. At the end of the fall semester, I again went to see my advisor, to plan the rest of the classes I needed for my degree. I got a surprising response. When he learned my name, he asked if I was related to Albert Hagan. I told him that Al was my older brother. Al was working as a county extension agent. My advisor informed me that due to state regulations, I could not work in the same state as another family member employed in extension, but I could go to Nebraska or another state. Moving to another state was unappealing. Again, I went back to my advisor. This time he suggested majoring in Agriculture Education. I met the advisor over the Agricultural Education Department, Dr. Dickenson. He was a kindly, motivational man who seemed very interested in me. I became enthused about Agriculture Education and once again changed my major.

In addition to the agriculture and education classes I was enrolled in at the university, I took a five-hour correspondence course in math from Kirksville Teachers College. There was just one reason to take the correspondence class.

I did not want to repeat the math class, with the same teacher who had failed me while I was in the hospital. In spite of this incredible overload of classes, and working many hours, by the end of the semester I had passed all the classes and made just enough money to pay for the next semester's tuition fees. I had a pay increase at the library along with new responsibilities. The head librarian put me in charge of the library circulation desk. I held this job during both my junior and senior years. What a timely blessing. This job not only paid my way through the rest of college, but allowed me to get greatly needed rest at night.

The summer after my junior year, I enrolled in Kirksville Teachers College, in Kirksville, Missouri. This was necessary to pick up the specific classes I needed, including more hours in math, because I couldn't get them at the university that summer. With the four courses I took that summer in Kirksville, I was able to finish all my education coursework requirements the next year as a senior.

My older brother, Raycel lived on the farm with my parents, until he married a wonderful lady, Miss Ruby Brown in 1938. He farmed "on the shares" with our dad, Ross, like Ross did with his dad, Robert. Raycel had an excellent hard work ethic and a love of farming. He worked hard to put in all of Dad's crops. Between semesters, I went home to help out on the farm. The economy was still in dreadful shape.

During my senior year, I lived in a small apartment with my youngest brother, Darrell. It was wonderful to have him in my life again. I had missed his contagious laughter and quick sense of humor. I was very busy with an overload of classes and work. Darrell was not taking as many classes, or working as many hours, during his first semester at the university. He wanted to be sure he got a successful start in college. I was able to show him around campus and Columbia. I took him to the Dixie Café for a burger, and gave him a tour of the library. I made coffee for him every morning before leaving for my first class. He washed the coffee pot every night before he went to bed. This went on for nearly four months. One day I told him we were out of coffee and he needed to stop by the store and get more if he wanted me to keep making coffee. He said he did not drink coffee. I did not drink coffee either. So we decided to quit making coffee and pouring it out.

Fall semester of my senior year, I was assigned to student teach one week before and several weeks after the semester started. Along with two other student teachers, I was sent to the high school, in Salisbury, Missouri. We were required to be there one week ahead of the students. The first few days, we followed the vocational agriculture teacher, as he showed us how he visited students on their farms and advised each one on their projects. The next week classes started. The teacher organized a field trip to take a large group of students to East St. Louis to a marketing day. We were required to go with him. The students were taking livestock to market. I became very sick to my stomach and could not go to St. Louis with them. The instructor told me to stay at the school and supervise the remaining classes. I got along very well. The superintendent checked on me several times. I don't think he knew I was aware of that.

After I finished with student teaching, I went back to school at Columbia. Every once in a while I would become sick again. I went to a doctor at the university clinic. To my dismay, he said my tonsils needed to be removed. I waited until I could miss a few classes. After mentioning my plans to Darrell, I checked into the university clinic for a tonsillectomy. It was free to students because the medical students needed practice. There were three other students waiting to be operated on that morning.

The doctor seemed irritated when the nurse took me into the operating room for surgery. Apparently, he was having a bad day and was feeling rushed. He slammed my head back and angrily told me to open my mouth. He started poking around in my mouth with a hooked instrument. I started to raise my head and close my mouth because he was hurting me. He took the palm of his hand and pushed my head back, then yelled, "Don't you move, and keep your mouth open!" He ordered the nurses to hold my hands. There was a nurse on both sides of me. One nurse told me to open my mouth. He reached into my mouth with an instrument which had two circle-shaped blades on one end, and a long handle which moved one of the circular blades. He pulled on my tonsil and then used the blade to cut it off. He didn't give me anything to stop the searing pain. When the doctor cut off my tonsil I squeezed one of the nurse's hands so hard that she screamed and dropped to the floor. I was in so much pain, I didn't realize what I was doing.

When she got up, she took hold of my arm with both hands. The doctor reached in and did the same thing to my remaining tonsil. When he was finished, they took me out to the recovery room. The doctor did this procedure to at least one other student. We were in the recovery room together. Neither of us could talk and had blood all over our mouths. I saw that student later and he described what they had done to him. The doctor hadn't given either of us anything for the pain. After my tonsils were removed, I did not get sick anymore, so in the end, it probably was a good thing.

Darrell spent a great deal of time socializing and playing badminton and horseshoes in our back yard after his classes. I thought I had better give him a little direction on how to be successful in college. The next time we were able to share a meal, which he had time to cook, I offered a little brotherly advice. I explained that college professors were stricter than high school teachers, that perfect attendance and a great deal of reading and studying were necessary to make good grades. I indicated that I was concerned he had so much free time. Perhaps he should consider studying more. Darrell good-naturedly said he was doing fine, and I had no need to worry about him. At the end of the semester Darrell had earned top grades in all of his classes. In fact, he made better grades than I did. I decided he might not need any more of my sage advice.

By this time, Darrell and I had a radio. He listened to the news every day, and I did when I had time. Darrell was extremely concerned about a recession, which caused unemployment to rise to nineteen percent. We discussed the effect this had on us, and our parents' farm. The law changed, which meant the minimum hourly wage was forty cents per hour for a forty-four hour workweek. That was more than we were making on our part-time jobs. I told Darrell it did not matter what we made, we were blessed to have any kind of job. We were getting by on what God gave us. I remember paying five dollars for a blanket that fall. It was a big investment for me.

On October 30th, Orson Welles' radio dramatization of "War of The Worlds" caused panic when it was broadcast. It sounded more like a breaking news story than a play. Darrell and I laughed that so many people were fooled into believing the prank. Orson Welles was severely criticized for this. The innocent people in our nation were learning not to believe everything they heard on the radio.

I enrolled in twenty-one hours both semesters of my senior year. One semester I had two classes at exactly the same time. I had a good friend in one of those classes. He took meticulous notes and studied with me, so that I could attend the other class. He even answered for me when the professor took attendance. I attended that class a few times, but not often. In the middle of the semester, I got a letter from the dean of the Department of Agriculture asking me to report to his office. It scared me. Why would he want to see me? It reminded me of the time in high school when the principal summoned me to his office. When I went to the meeting, he asked a few questions. He pointed out that my records showed I was taking two courses at the same time. He asked me how that was possible. I told him, "It's not easy." He slowly smiled and replied he did not think it would be easy. I explained that I had changed my major to education. To get the required courses before graduation, I had to take both classes at the same time, because that was the only time they were offered that year. I suddenly remembered a moment from my childhood when Reva and I told my mother a story about paint on Reva's dress. I looked the dean squarely in the eyes and truthfully told him how my friend spoke up for me during roll call and shared his class notes. The dean did not make me withdraw from the course.

The class I rarely attended was a dairy production course. The professor said it was all theory and he would teach out of the textbook that he had written. I read the book a few times and studied the notes my friend shared. The evening before the final I slept for two hours, then studied all night until seven the next morning. I passed the test and received an "S" for the course. I thanked the Lord when I passed all my classes that semester.

I was able to graduate in 1939, with a Bachelor of Science in Agriculture Education. However, I did not graduate until the end of the summer term, because I had changed my major and needed to take a few extra classes.

I proudly wore the same suit for my college graduation that I had worn for my high school graduation. I graduated in four years even though I missed an entire semester and worked many hours. Most amazing of all, and solely by the grace of God, I had graduated without a school loan debt and without financial help from anyone.

I reminisced about the advice from my high school teachers and the sarcastic banker in Princeton. It seemed impossible that was only four years earlier; I had surely grown and aged in many ways. The Lord had given direction, and although it made no sense to anyone else, He indeed had a plan for my life.

My parents came down for my graduation. Reva and Charlie were also there, as they had moved to Columbia. I was honored to share the day with them. I considered graduation day a victory for the Lord.

1939 Graduation from Missouri University;
Pearle Hagan, Raymond Hagan, Ross Hagan

Raymond Hagan in 1939

The Children of Ross and Pearle Hagan

1. Jesse Delores Hagan graduated from Mercer High School and married Lawrence LaFollette November 25, 1926
2. Albert Ross Hagan graduated from Princeton High School, and earned a BS, MS, and PHD. He married Melva Snodgrass April 11, 1937
3. Raycel Shirley Hagan attended Mercer high school then successfully farmed the Hagan Farm. He married Ruby Brown December 10, 1938
4. Vee Marie Hagan graduated from Princeton High School and completed College classes at Maryville. She married William Alley November 7, 1933
5. Raymond Dale Hagan graduated from Princeton High School, and earned a BSE, MSE and completed further graduate studies at University of Michigan. He married Valetta Juanita Wharton (Nita) on March 7, 1942
6. Reva Pearle Hagan graduated from Princeton High School, then married Charles Cornett on September 3, 1935
7. William Robert Darrell Hagan graduated from Princeton High School and earned a BS and MS. He married Betty Ellis November 1943

Chapter 17

THE UNEXPECTED

In 1939, thirty-three people graduated from the University of Missouri with a degree qualifying them to be vocational agriculture instructors. Sadly there were only three openings in the entire state of Missouri in this field. In June, I decided to take a few summer classes and work full-time at the university library.

I did not apply for a job teaching, but I did have two interviews. Eagleville High School in Eagleville, Missouri had an open teaching position and called back three candidates to have a second interview. I was one of the three. The three of us drove together to the interview, and discussed the position that was available. One of the other applicants chosen for the second interview was my best friend Joe Campbell. He said he would like to get the job because he was raised nearby. Jack Tanner, another friend of mine, was the third graduate riding with us.

When arrived at Eagleville School, we discovered there were others waiting to be interviewed. We were instructed to draw numbers out of a hat to determine who would be interviewed first, second and so forth. One of the board members for the school district was a county agent who had grown up in Mercer County. He lived next door to my sister, Reva during our senior year in high school. He remembered me and was very friendly during my interview.

I wanted my friend Joe to get the job, so during my interview I talked positively about him. Each time I was asked a question, I would tell him that I was capable, but that Joe Campbell was even better in that area. The county agent asked if I was trying to get the job, or trying to get it for Joe. I told him I would like the job, but since Joe was raised in the area, the teaching situation would be a perfect fit for him.

Later we found out the school had hired a teacher before those interviews took place. They had interviewed us to give us experience. The new teacher's name was Andy White. We worked together a few years later. Joe Campbell did get a teaching position, however it was in Illinois. Before long, his home school at Ridgeway, Missouri, had an opening in vocational agriculture. I was delighted when he got this position and was able to teach in his hometown.

The day after summer school was over, I began to think seriously about what I should do with my life now that college was finished. I met a friend downtown, who also graduated recently. We sat on the curb while we talked. We thought it was funny that we were both just beginning to think about what we were going to do for a living. Jobs were not plentiful at that time because our country was still in midst of the Great Depression, but we still weren't concerned. We had already accomplished our huge objective; graduation from college.

I was temporarily staying with my sister, Reva and her husband, Charlie. When I went home that afternoon, a letter was waiting on the table for me, from the American Agricultural Chemical Company in East St. Louis, Illinois. The letter asked if I would be interested in a position in their laboratory. This was completely unexpected. I had no idea why I received the letter, but thought it may not be too bad to work for them. It was a job, after all. The letter contained a phone number. I called immediately to set up an interview.

In August of 1939, wearing my graduation suit, I hitchhiked to St. Louis for the interview. When I reached the Mississippi River, I discovered I had to pay a dollar to cross the bridge to get to East St. Louis, Illinois. I did not have a dollar. I had no idea what to do to get across the bridge. I said a prayer asking God for help. I walked a little way down the first street I came to. There was a line of men begging for money. They were all sitting on the ground with their hats held out. I went up to the first man. I asked if he would give me a dollar to get across the bridge. Amazingly, he gave it to me. I thanked him and left a little dazed. I had just been given money from a beggar.

I finally crossed the bridge and continued walking until I found the American Agricultural Chemical Company. I met the man who sent me the letter. He was friendly and interviewed me for nearly an hour. He gave me a tour of the facility. The tour was very interesting, and convinced me I would enjoy working for this company. He asked me to start immediately. I told him that I had not brought even one change of clothing. He needed me to work and was not concerned with my clothing situation. I started work the same day. My new supervisor put me up at his home until I could rent a room. At the end of the week I hitchhiked back to Columbia to gather my belongings. I was still able to fit all I owned into the one dollar suitcase my parents had given me four years earlier. I said

The unexpected

goodbye to my sister, Reva, Charlie and my darling niece, Ann and hitchhiked back to East St. Louis, Illinois.

American Agriculture Chemical Company was located near the river in an industrial area, so there were no residential areas close by. Because I did not own a vehicle, I had to ride busses and streetcars to go to work. Some days I was able to ride with the man who was head of manufacturing. This was an incredible lifestyle change from my life on the farm, and in the small town of Columbia, Missouri. I met people with diverse backgrounds and beliefs in this big city. By observing them, I learned many life lessons that helped me avoid mistakes in the years ahead.

American Agriculture Chemical Company was a large company manufacturing fertilizers and other chemical products. I was hired to be a chemist. We tested batches of fertilizer to determine the level of chemicals in them, such as nitrogen and potassium. This process took several days using the method the lead chemist implemented to perform the test. After using the prescribed method for a while, I was able to develop a shorter process. By eliminating several steps in the procedure, the test would produce the same results in just two or three hours. I liked the challenging work.

The head chemist was an interesting man. He truly enjoyed his job, and working with him was a pleasure. He graduated from the University of Missouri a few years ahead of me. I found out that he remembered me from our chemistry classes at the university, and recommended me to be interviewed for the position.

Each morning I stopped at a store on my way to work and picked up a little carton of milk to drink with my lunch. I noticed a time or two that my milk was missing when we sat down for lunch. I found out later the head chemist had gotten in my lunch box, took the carton of milk and drank it. He was not trying to hide it from me. He just never told me he was doing it. When I asked him about it, he said, "Yeah, it's good milk." He brought coffee every day in a container to drink with his lunch. One day he was late for lunch, so I decided I would drink it. It was strong and black. I liked my coffee with cream and sugar. I found sugar in his lunch box, so I was able to get the coffee down. He didn't say anything about it that day, so I did it several more times in the coming weeks. Finally, he called my hand on that, but it was all in fun. He told me if I quit drinking his coffee, he would quit drinking my milk. I agreed to the deal. I enjoyed his offbeat sense of humor.

The head sales representative for our company was a good looking man, but extremely aggressive and somewhat unfriendly. He was a former University of Missouri professor. Since he sold the fertilizer, he needed to know the precise measurements of all the chemicals. There were ten other lab employees working with me. They kept their distance from him. The man in charge of testing would send me to the sales representative with the new batch of fertilizer samples. His little office was in a corner, surrounded by glass, so he could watch everyone working. The employees would not talk or look around. They were fearful he would think they were not working. When I took samples to him, it was all business, without even a smile. One day I took a sample to him that did not test as he desired. It was a chemical mix that had not been made correctly in production. We had tested it three times, with the same outcome. I showed him the results. He said the mix had to be right and the test must be wrong. I told him the test was correct. He pointed his finger at me and in a very gruff voice said, "You need to take that and test it again!" I looked him straight in the eyes and pointed my finger back at him and said very loudly: "We already tested it three times and the results are correct!" He was taken off guard that someone was talking back to him. He immediately quieted down and said that we needed to do something about that batch. When I exited his office, the employees stared at me as if they were in shock. After that confrontation, he was always very nice to me. I thought afterwards that I stood up to him because I was not concerned about keeping the job. I knew I was going to get a teaching position eventually. From that day on, he was friendlier to me and everyone else.

On September 1st of 1939, the newspapers and radio stations made a shocking announcement. Nazi Germany attacked Poland. Then France, Australia and the United Kingdom declared war on Germany. I was astounded that seemingly overnight our world could be in a total uproar. The United States decided to remain neutral. I was thankful for that, as we were still in a very depressed economy, and things were just beginning to look a little brighter. During the next few months, our country began re-arming for war, "just in case" we needed to defend ourselves. This provided jobs, which helped ease the economic depression.

I kept a record of my income and expenditures beginning in 1939. When I put gas in someone's car it cost ten cents a gallon. A loaf of bread was eight cents, unless I bought day old bread. It was one cent less. I have always enjoyed having toast for breakfast. A new toaster cost nearly sixteen dollars. I decided to save for one. I looked at a new car, but could not afford one, as it would cost around $700.

My wonderful, fun-loving grandfather, William Riley Shirley, passed into heaven October 9, 1939. I was in high school when he had a stroke, leaving him unable to walk. He spent the remaining years of his life in a wheelchair. My grandmother was getting older and was somewhat frail, but my Aunt Gertrude took excellent care of Granddad at home on their farm, during all the years he was incapacitated. Today, he would have gone to a nursing home, and likely

The unexpected

would not have lived as long. Throughout his illness, he maintained his wonderful sense of humor and was an encouragement to everyone around him. The influence he provided during my childhood and youth gave me confidence to take on the difficult circumstances in my life. I knew this kindhearted man loved me. He believed I could do anything. My sweet mother was sad over the loss of her wonderful father. I wrote frequent letters to her, telling her about my new life in the big city, in hopes it would help ease her grief.

I had stayed with the head of manufacturing for the first few weeks I was in East St. Louis. He soon found a place for me to rent close to his house. Another man was renting a room there when I moved in. I rented the room from a nice couple. I thought they were quite old, but they were probably only in their fifties. He had an excellent job as manager of a daily newspaper. I knew he was making good money. His wife did not work outside the home.

Since I did not know anyone other than my coworkers, the couple I was renting from introduced me to a friend. My new friend and I went to the horse races in Illinois that fall. There were eight or nine races every afternoon. Many people went there to watch the races and some would place a bet. I only bet a few times, since I did not have much money. I enjoyed watching the races. The horses were beautiful, and I would have loved riding them. The horse races stopped for the season in late September. The next summer, my friend and I went back to the races.

The couple I was staying with began having domestic issues. I could tell it was getting serious. One day the man came to me and said I should start looking for another place to live. He said, "We're losing our house." I did not understand. He explained that his wife had been going to the horse races and losing money. They were greatly in debt and unable pay for the house. I was astounded that such a nice lady could selfishly allow a recreational activity to ruin their lives.

This conversation made me think carefully about what I had been doing for enjoyment. I had kept track of every penny I spent. I calculated that including bus fares, meals, and occasionally betting on the horses, I had spent fifty dollars during the two seasons I went to the races. I decided I would not go any more, and planned to tell my friend when we met on Saturday. I had been watching the statistical records for the horses, though. On my last day at the track I made one final bet. I was astounded when my horse won the race and the money I won reimbursed me for all I had spent over two seasons, and even fifty dollars ahead. Suddenly, I understood what had caused the nice landlady to become addicted to gambling. I learned a lesson about staying focused on doing what is right. In spite of the winnings, I have not gambled since that day. I saw a verse in my Bible from Proverbs 13:11 and marked it. "Money that comes easily disappears quickly, but money that is gathered little by little will grow."

I moved to a boarding house managed by an older man and woman. It was a "room and board" type of place. They had four boarders living with them. This was a common practice in the Depression years. Running a boarding house provided steady income for people who owned their homes. One of the boarders was a man who had worked for the railroad all of his life. He was within two or three years of retirement. He sincerely hated his job and complained constantly. He taught me another life lesson. I decided if I ever had a job that made me miserable, I would quit, even if it meant starving to death. Fortunately, I never had a job I did not like.

After riding the bus on my way home from work, I walked the last few blocks. Each day I saw a young man riding a motorcycle. It looked like great fun, and I considered purchasing one. We seemed to meet at the same corner every day. Several times he took the turn a little too fast for my comfort. One day the wheels went out from under him. He and the motorcycle slid all the way across the intersection and into the bank across the road. He was seriously injured. I decided I could live without a motorcycle.

I frequently went to the YMCA and enjoyed playing various sports like badminton. At the YMCA, I met a man near my age, who owned a car. He seemed like a nice person and we became friends. We went to the Illinois State Fair, and he frightened me with his reckless driving. We double dated a few times, once with a couple of girls we met at the YMCA. They lived on the west side of St. Louis. The ladies did not live at the same location, so he dropped me and my date off at her place and said he would return to pick me up later. At midnight, he still had not come. I had to take the bus all the way back to East St. Louis. While waiting for the bus, I stepped in the doorway of a bar, to keep out of the freezing wind. Several men burst through the door of the bar, onto the sidewalk, fighting and yelling obscenities. I decided that neighborhood was not a good place to be at night. I was learning not to trust everyone, as I was accustomed to doing at home in North Missouri.

One of the most enjoyable experiences I had in St Louis was the opportunity to go to the professional baseball games. This was something I had only dreamed about. I really enjoyed watching the Cardinals' and Browns' games. The Cardinals were a top major league team at the time. In 1940, the Cardinals' win/loss record was 84-69 during the season and they finished third in the National League. Although they were not a major league team, I enjoyed going to the Browns' games and getting acquainted with the players. I remembered one pitcher, Bobo Newsom, was outstanding enough to be in the major leagues, but at the time players of African-American descent were not allowed.

The unexpected

I followed his career and frequently heard his name on the radio. For years he remained a top pitcher.

I tried to settle into life in the city, but in my heart I remained a country boy. I prayed about living the rest of my life in the city, or finding a way to return to the country life I longed for. I had been exposed to many new activities, and many kinds of people in St. Louis. I learned a lot about life, both good and bad. I discovered firsthand that many of the values and ideas my mother had taught me in Sunday school at Bethel Church were excellent guidelines to follow.

In December of 1940, I heard from college friends about a teaching position in vocational agriculture that was coming open at a small school south of Sedalia, in Green Ridge, Missouri. I decided to check on this opening. In a phone call, the superintendent encouraged me to come see their facility. That weekend I hitchhiked to Columbia where my brother Albert was working. Albert was doing very well and had purchased a car. On Monday, he drove me down to Green Ridge for the interview. I spoke with the superintendent and toured the school. Green Ridge was a small town of about three hundred people. It seemed very small after living in East St. Louis. I thought it would be all right since the vocational agriculture program was very good. The superintendent offered to pay me $1,800 a year, which was $600 more than the other high school teachers were making. The pay was higher because vocational agriculture teachers worked many extra hours outside of school, visiting farms where the students were living, and leading the FFA. I told the superintendent that I was very interested in the job, and would call him the next day to let him know my decision. Albert and I discussed this opportunity, as well as my current job, on the way back to Columbia. He gave me gentle, but good advice, concerning my future. My kindhearted big brother was always supportive when I needed him.

I planned to turn in my resignation when I returned to St. Louis. When I told my immediate supervisors about my plans to leave, I found out they wanted me to stay. They sent me see to the grumpy head salesman. He asked what my teaching salary would be at Green Ridge. When I said, "Eighteen hundred a year," he boldly offered me five times that amount to stay at American Agricultural Chemical Company as a salesman. He wanted to train me in sales. I would make more in this position than being a chemist. It was a difficult decision, so I told him that I needed time to consider my options. The amount of money he offered was astounding, and I assure you, very tempting. I carefully weighed each alternative in my mind. I always prayed about decisions I had to make. Three days later, I turned in my resignation. I went to college to be a vocational agriculture teacher and I felt the Lord was leading me in that direction.

Chapter 18

INSPIRING OTHERS TO EXCELLENCE

In December of 1940, I was excited to begin teaching at Green Ridge, Missouri. The school district scheduled the last week of December for Christmas break. The time off gave me an opportunity to visit my parents on Christmas and move my meager belongings to Green Ridge. Everything still fit in the suitcase my parents gave me after high school graduation. Back on the farm, things were changing. In the early 1940s, my family's farm was the first in Mercer County to get electricity. Dad and area farmers ran Rural Electrification Administration (REA) electric lines nineteen miles to the Hagan farm. That was an exciting time in the Hagan house. Raycel was "farming on the shares" with Dad, just as my dad had done with his father. They were an unbeatable team.

Being reunited with my family that Christmas was heartwarming. We had a few days to catch up on each other's lives. Family is family, whether you have been separated ten years, or ten days. Together we prayed, cried, laughed, spoke of our political views, and allowed ourselves to feel the happiness of acceptance and belonging. With each smile, joke, and story I felt a connection that I had almost forgotten after so many years apart. I cherish those memories. I can still see the love and happiness in my parents' faces. I left for my newest adventure in life feeling refreshed and renewed.

Because very few rental properties existed in Green Ridge, I was grateful to rent the same room as the previous teacher. Mr. and Mrs. Ream were also thankful to rent a bedroom and share their meals with me. They were a kindly couple and needed a few extra dollars to pay their bills. Mrs. Ream was a very good cook, so I was contented living in their home. My predecessor left the area because he took a position in Kansas City. The new job provided a car for him to drive. He offered to sell me his current vehicle, a 1939 Ford. I would be required to make visits to the farms of my students, so I accepted his offer. It was the first car I owned. He was a nice man and allowed me a few months before I was required to pay for the car. The Lord was again providing for all my needs. I believed this was confirmation that I had made the right career move.

On the first day of school in January 1941, I learned the vocational agriculture students were divided into two class levels. Freshmen and sophomores were in class together and juniors and seniors were grouped together.

I walked anxiously into the junior and senior class. There were sixteen students. They were casually visiting, leaning against the walls, or sitting on tables. I asked everyone to take a seat. They informed me they did not sit in chairs or at desks during class, but worked in groups and discussed various subjects.

During lunch, I spoke with a fellow teacher about the previous teacher's methods. I confided I did not understand how students could learn with such confusion in the classroom. He replied it would be impossible for him to teach effectively in that setting, even though it worked well for the gentleman I replaced. I decided I would have an organized classroom, and promptly made a seating chart.

When the students came to class the next day, I asked them to sit in assigned seats. Again, they informed me they did not sit in chairs in agriculture class. Choosing to remain calm, I explained that I needed to get acquainted with them and it would be easier for me to learn their names if they were in assigned seats. Next, I asked them to take notes. Most students did not bring school supplies to agriculture class. Much to their surprise, I passed out textbooks and gave them assignments. Some of the students did a little work, others did none. A few days later, I handed out assignment sheets and reference books. I told them that we would soon have a discussion. It took half of the semester and a lot of patience to get the students accustomed to my teaching style.

I could tell my students did not like me very well, mainly because I required them to work in a traditional classroom setting. Near the semester's end in late January, I prepared the students for the upcoming final exams. On the last day of the semester, I wrote questions on the chalkboard. I asked them to take out paper and pencil to begin answering the essay questions. The students crossed their arms and sat looking at me. They refused to take the exam. Knowing I was being brazenly challenged, I sternly told them it was time to begin the test. One of the bolder students declared they did not do that in agriculture class. I told him that I was the teacher now and the grade they made on the test would go on their report card. They did not like it, but realized I was serious. Some students began writing. One student, Julian, came to me and said he was sick. He asked if he could take the test the next day. I said that was acceptable. He never returned to take the final exam. He was the son of the school board president.

The high school grade cards were passed from one teacher to the next, after entering the grades for each student in their class. I gave everyone in my class an "M" on their report cards, except the boy who chose not to take the final. Since I was only there a few weeks before the end of semester, I had very little data for their grades. Julian came to me with his grade card and said he could not take it home with an "F" on it. He told me he always received "E"s and demanded I change his grade. I explained that he needed to apply himself next semester and if I saw improvement, I would consider giving him an "E." He took the grade card, and as he walked out, threatened to send his mom to speak with me.

I did not think much about his threat. In fact, I had forgotten about it until I walked into my classroom the following morning. Julian's mother was sitting on my desk. I immediately recognized this as an attempt to intimidate me. I chose to face the threatening situation head on. I began the conversation before she could speak. I stated that I realized her son intended to go to college, and he always made "E"s. I explained that Julian was not an "E" student and he would have difficulties in college, unless he learned to study and earn his grades now. She bristled and did not agree with me. I kindly explained that she had a fine son and I was interested in helping him improve his study habits. She finally agreed we would work together. Relief flooded my mind. I spoke with a trusted fellow teacher about the incident. He was shocked I stood up to Julian's mother. The superintendent had told all the teachers to give him an "E" no matter what Julian actually earned. As a new staff member, I was unaware of this directive. I did not want to have trouble with the school board one month into my teaching career. I hoped everything would be all right since Julian's mother seemingly was no longer upset. In time, Julian and I gained respect for one another and became very good friends.

Mr. and Mrs. Ream and I ate dinner together nearly every evening. We often listened to radio news while we ate. It was obvious the world was in great turmoil. The war was increasing. Adolph Hitler was an evil aggressor to many nations. He targeted Jewish people as enemies. We heard Winston Churchill in a worldwide broadcast tell the United States to show its support by sending arms to the British. He said, "Give us the tools, and we will finish the job!" Mr. Ream was a great fan of Mr. Churchill. He wrote this quote down and read it out loud to me several times. Like most of our nation, Mr. Ream was in favor of sending weapons, but not in committing our military.

After the semester started, I involved my students in the local and district FFA contests that were held each spring. When my students began to show interest, I took them on a field trip. At last, I felt I was connecting with them. I wanted to inspire each student to do his best in every situation.

Before the state competitions in April, I took my classes to a nearby farm. The purpose was to teach the students to judge and place cattle. The practical lessons were effective. I took my top twelve students to the state competitions at the University of Missouri. We stayed with my sister, Reva and her husband, Charlie, in Columbia, Missouri. Thirteen of us slept on the floor in their small home because we had no money for a motel. I suspect my sweet sister was glad when the rowdy teenage boys were gone. Regardless of how old we were, my siblings and I retained close family ties, supporting each other when possible. To my delight, we returned home to Green Ridge High School with the trophy for the grand champion judging team. I felt I was gaining respect, not only from my students, but from fellow educators and the community as well.

Influenza quickly spread through our school and community in the spring of 1941. One of my students, Ernest, was very ill. The doctor did not expect him to live much longer. One of the coaches was aware of my experience with influenza and dust pneumonia a few years earlier. He suggested I visit Ernest and the grandmother raising him. I did not want to go alone, so I asked my friend Julian to accompany me. I picked him up and drove to Ernest's farm. When his grandmother answered the door, I asked to see him. She informed us he was not doing well and repeatedly declared she knew he was going to die. Again, I asked if we could see him. Finally, she permitted us to come in and took us to him. He was in a bed in the corner of the living room. I am certain he heard our conversation. He was colorless and lying very still. He opened his eyes slightly when I told him who I was. He knew Julian well. I asked how he was feeling. He said he did not feel well and knew he was going to die.

I noticed his eyes were alert. I reached down and took hold of his arm to take his pulse. I was encouraged that his pulse was strong. I told him that he had a strong pulse rate. Again, he said he was going to die. I laid my ear on his chest and could hear that he was breathing well. I knew the pneumonia was not bad. I sat a few minutes then looked in his eyes and asked, "Ernest, do you want to die?" He replied, "No Mr. Hagan, but I know I am going to." He told me he was not eating or drinking because everything tasted bad.

I told him of my experience years earlier. "Ernest, when I was in college, I got pneumonia, just like you have now. The doctors believed I could not get well. I started eating and drinking a little bit, then moving around a little. Soon I was feeling better. Ernest, I sincerely believe you can get over this pneumonia too." I explained he needed to eat and drink every time his grandmother brought him something, no matter how bad it tasted. I asked if he thought he could do that. He said he would try. The longer Julian and I chatted with Ernest, the more he was willing to talk. He even sounded more energetic. I wanted this young man to thrive and enjoy a wonderful life.

As we were leaving, his grandmother walked out behind us. She thanked us for coming, even though she was still convinced he was going to die. I told her she needed to encourage him to eat and make very sure he was drinking often. I also told her that she had said he was going to die at least a dozen times while we were there and gave her strict instructions to stop saying those words. I firmly told her she must tell him he was looking better, and she could see that he was feeling better. She had to boost his confidence. I hoped we had inspired him to choose to live. That night I prayed, asking the Lord to heal Ernest.

A few days later I learned he was indeed feeling better. His parents came to see him. Ernest told them about my visit and our conversation. News of my visit with Ernest and his grandmother spread throughout the community. He was able to return to school that spring. I had done something good for Ernest. Soon others in the community were seeking my advice for their problems. This happened on a daily basis. It was a bit scary, but I was thankful for the opportunity to help people in time of need. Several families began inviting me to dinner in their homes. All of these families just happened to have young, single daughters. It did not take me long to realize what was going on. I was working a steady job, with a decent income, which was uncommon in this community. The Depression was getting better, but jobs were still difficult to find.

I decided to start a night class for the young men in the community. Many had grown up as farmers, but had lost their family farms in the dirty thirties. These young men returned to Green Ridge after working whatever jobs they could find in other locations. They came home looking for a way to start over. I called my class the Young Farmers Group.

Young Farmers Group, Green Ridge, Missouri 1941

One night, when the Young Farmers Group was over, the school custodian asked to speak with me. He was distraught. His old dairy cow was down and about to die. I had grown to like this goodhearted man. I asked him a few questions and arrived at the conclusion his cow had milk fever. He did not have money to call a veterinarian in from Sedalia. He asked if I would help him. I was tired after a long day, but could not turn him down. I waited for the Young Farmers Group members to leave, then went to the athletic department. I found a needle and hand pump used for inflating basketballs. I followed the custodian to his home. His sick cow was in his old barn. We tied her head securely. As he held her, I stuck the needle in each teat, on the udder of the cow. I used the pump to blow her udder up tight. We tied the end of each teat with a string to hold in the air. I had never done this, but I knew from my university classes, theoretically it was a possible cure for milk fever. I gave him instructions to release the air when she showed signs of recovery. There were other treatments, but I did not have access to the medication. The custodian let me know the cow had recovered. I'm not sure what a veterinarian would have done, but I found out a shot of calcium gluconate in a blood vessel would cure milk fever.

My vocational agriculture students told me the previous teacher had taken them on a trip to Tennessee. After a great deal of contemplation, I decided to take my interested students to Colorado. Due to the Depression, many students had never been out of the county. In fact, I had never traveled this far from home. This would be an excellent opportunity to learn about other states, see farmland in Kansas, Colorado, and experience camping. I invited students from all grades in my high school classes and the men from my Young Farmers Group to take part in this adventure. Thirty-two of us made the trip. The superintendent allowed us to use a school bus and an experienced driver. I planned to lead the bus in my car, pulling a trailer. The trailer was equipped with a kerosene cook stove and cooking implements, so we could prepare our meals. Each person brought a bedroll. We planned to camp out every night. Our trip was scheduled to begin after the school year ended in 1941.

When the big day arrived, thirty excited young men assembled at the high school. The bus driver and I were ready with a carefully planned route marked on maps. After a long and hot drive through the state of Kansas, we cheered when we saw the Colorado state line. The first place we visited in Colorado was the Garden of the Gods in Colorado Springs. Pike's Peak was clearly visible. The students were excited to see such a tall mountain. Of course, they wanted to go to the top of Pike's Peak. The students clamored to join tours to the mountaintop in special trams. The trams did not have a roof, so people could stand up to get a better view of everything. I decided I would drive my car up the mountain, with a few students riding with me. The remaining students went on the tram with our bus driver. I soon realized I never wanted to drive up that mountain again. The roads were narrow and poorly constructed. They zigzagged up the mountain with frequent blind corners and dizzying drop-offs. It was frightening to get close to the edge of the mountain when meeting a car coming from the opposite direction. Sometimes drivers would not go to their side of the road because they were frightened by the steep cliffs. We had to stop and add water to the radiator several times because this steep drive was hard on the engine. Many cars were overheating. We finally got to the top and met the rest of our group. The magnificent views were breathtaking. We stayed on top of the mountain only a short time. We recognized we could not tarry long in the high altitude, because the air was thin. We were getting dizzy. All too soon it was time to go back down that mountain. I was praying the breaks on my car would hold.

After I recovered from the wild drive up and down Pike's Peak, we drove toward Cripple Creek, Colorado. Along the way we dangled our feet in babbling brooks, but not for long because the water was freezing. When we got close to Cripple Creek, it was late in the evening. We discovered the sun sets very quickly in the mountains. I told our bus driver to find a level place to park the bus, while I went into town to buy groceries. He remained parked near the highway and supervised the students. I was planning to look for a place we could stay that night. I took three students with me. It was a very small town, but thankfully, there was a grocery store. While walking to the grocery store, some teenagers joined arms, blocking the sidewalk in front of the grocery store. I knew they were daring us to walk through them. I quickly guided my boys into the street and whispered for them not to talk. The teenagers did not bother us. We walked into the store and saw a man standing next to a wood stove, by the back wall. He had two guns and a badge. An older woman was with him. They looked and acted extremely drunk. These were not the kinds of experiences I wanted my students to have. We found the necessary groceries and quickly went to the cash register. I told the cashier what kind of group we were with and inquired if he knew a place we could stay for the night. He warned me to not stay close to town because the locals would torment us. We took the groceries back to the bus and started over the mountain. I prayed for the Lord to help us find a safe place for my boys.

We did a lot of mountain driving on the trip, but neither the bus driver, nor I, had driven in mountains at night. We were worried because it was getting dark and we knew little about where we were going. Finally, we saw a gas station. I decided we should fill up our tanks. In Missouri a gallon of gas cost twelve cents, but in Colorado we had to pay seventeen cents a gallon. I told the attendant where we were from. He said he grew up in Sedalia and had lived in Colorado for the past twenty-seven years. He asked many questions about

Sedalia, including the price of gasoline. He was amazed how much his hometown had changed over the years. I asked if he knew a place we could stay that night. Because we were from his home state, he said we were welcome to sleep in a large, empty metal building in back of the gas station. It was perfect and right next to us. Another prayer was answered.

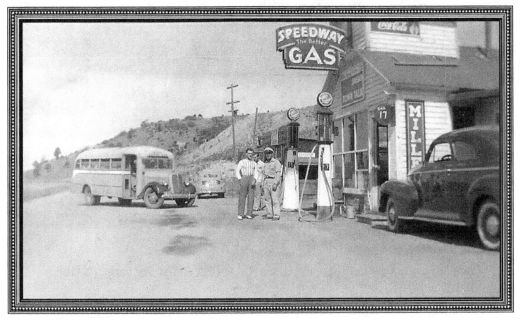

Summer of 1941 near Cripple Creek, Colorado

Throughout the trip, each of the boys helped with aspects of camping. This involved the preparation of food, cooking, washing dishes, and packing. At supper that evening, one student refused to help. I told him he could go home. I was instantly sorry for saying it, and relieved he decided to help. It was dark and cold, and certainly I would have gone after him. We had supper, and then slept in our warm, cozy quilts. The next morning we cooked our breakfast and continued our journey.

Summer of 1941
Camping out in Colorado with the Green Ridge FFA and Young Farmer's Group

I think finding that safe place to spend the night was the best part of our trip. After the stress of driving in the mountains at night, being rolled up in our quilts on the ground was a blessing. The Lord had protected us and then provided a safe place to spend the night.

Our trip was a huge success. We saw wonderful sights and beautiful mountain views. We observed livestock and farmland along the way. This was a magnificent learning experience for all of us. But best of all were the close relationships we developed. We became friends for life.

We arrived home safely at nine o'clock on a Friday night. I was so tired I could hardly see, but still took several of the young men home. I was pleased that many students had someone meet them at school to take them home. I was completely exhausted. When I made it back to the house where I was boarding, Mrs. Ream told me it was Friday, so I would not have to get up early the next day. I told her to not wake me because I was tired and just wanted to sleep and rest. I got up twice on Saturday to use the restroom and get a drink of water. I slept Friday night, Saturday, Saturday night, and most of Sunday. Being exhausted was well worth it, because we had a great trip, with memories to last a lifetime. I also learned something firsthand that I heard Granddad Hagan say many times. Missouri was one of the most beautiful places God created.

I planned various activities with the Young Farmers Group. We had boxing gloves, and sometimes during class break-time would allow those who were interested to box for a few minutes. It was an enjoyable and lighthearted activity. Because of this pastime activity, the young men wanted to have a boxing tournament at night and invite people from the community to attend. I considered it and finally agreed this would be a good money-making activity, if we charged a small admittance fee. We had several Young Farmers and some high school students signed up to box. I matched them according to their ability levels. We had fifteen pairs of boxers for the night of entertainment. We invited people from the community.

To my amazement, every seat in the auditorium was occupied that night, and others were standing. We introduced the boxers as they came forward to the ring. They would box three rounds. I was the referee. If it began to look like it was one-sided, I would stop the fight. The students were well matched. Our boxing gloves were large and safer than those used in professional boxing, but it was still possible to be injured. The last match showcased two boxers from my Young Farmers Group. One of them was obviously experienced. I matched him with a tall, active young man who I thought could keep up with him. His personality was somewhat abrasive. In hindsight, I realize the experienced boxer was delighted for the chance to box with him. He wanted to hurt the boy.

The tall young man was not well-liked. He was not only taller, but had very long arms. The experienced boxer had difficulty landing punches. I let them box the first round. The crowd was excited and cheered enthusiastically during the first round. At the start of the second round, the experienced boxer became more aggressive, landing a few hard punches. The crowd began wildly cheering him on. He landed a blow to his opponent's mouth, breaking a tooth and smashing his lip. Blood was squirting out of his lip. Of course, I got between them immediately.

I made a call to stop the fight. The injured man became irrational, yelling, "No, I'm not going to quit! I want to beat him up!" I adamantly yelled no, while restraining him. I finally stopped their bickering and got them off the floor and off the stage. The crowd went wild. They loved it. That was the most exciting part of the evening.

There were many fine, hardworking people in Green Ridge. I grew to love the small community and felt blessed to live and work there. Thinking back to my life in East St. Louis was like looking at two different worlds. I was much happier and more relaxed living in Green Ridge. I even felt healthier, perhaps from breathing fresh air and being outside more often.

One of the men I became acquainted with at church was a mailman. He started a small business hatching eggs and selling chickens. He kept building the business and soon needed larger facilities to keep up with the demand. He decided the best way to accommodate his thriving business was to build several large buildings just for hatching chickens. The location he chose was in the closest large town, Sedalia, Missouri. He asked me to help him build the buildings. We put up a large building and a hatchery. He soon mailed chickens all over the country. Even though he was very successful, he remained humble. He retained a small business in Green Ridge to benefit the local people. I admired his business acumen as well as his loyalty to our community.

Chapter 19

ONE + ONE = ONE

While helping my friend make plans for the new hatchery buildings, I met one of his employees, Virginia Wharton. We often ran into each other and enjoyed laughing and talking together. I took her to a movie one night, and then drove her home to the small town of LaMonte, Missouri, where she lived with her parents. When I dropped her off from our date, I met her sister, Juanita. The first time I saw "Nita," she was on the front porch swing with cold cream on her sunburned face. She had attended a ball game that day and was blistered from the sun. She was embarrassed and seemed quite shy. She was a pretty young woman with a quiet nature. I found out Nita was working at Rice Hatcheries in Sedalia, Missouri, as a bookkeeper. She lived in LaMonte with her parents and siblings. Virginia was younger and more outgoing than her sister, Nita. Virginia and I would sometimes take Nita and other friends with us to the movies, or dinner. One night I went to Virginia's workplace in Green Ridge to pick her up for a date, and she kept making excuses why she could not go out. She seemed to always be busy. I decided that I would drive to LaMonte and ask Nita to go to the movie. We saw "Citizen Kane." It was written and directed by Orson Welles. We had a great time together.

Nita and I began dating on weekends and occasionally met for dinner during the week. One of our favorite restaurants was Eddie's Drive In, on Highway 50, in Sedalia. They had something new called "fast food." We enjoyed hamburgers and french fried potatoes. I usually ordered chocolate milk. Each booth had a little jukebox for customers to listen to popular tunes. Nita and I liked "Chattanooga Choo Choo," but our favorite song was "Elmer's Tune." Both songs were recorded by the Glenn Miller Orchestra. When "Elmer's Tune" played on my car radio, we sang these words together, "Why are the stars always winkin' and blinkin' above? What makes a fella start thinkin' of fallin' in love? It's not the season, the reason, it's plain as the moon. It's just Elmer's tune." We always thought of each other when we heard that song. It became our special song.

Nita and Ray in front of Ray's first car

Virginia was soon transferred to the new hatchery in Sedalia. The sisters decided to get an apartment together in Sedalia and stop commuting from LaMonte every day. Nita and I now lived closer to each other, making it easier to get together. We grew close, looking forward to our time together, as we dated through the summer and fall of 1941.

We learned a horrific new word that summer–holocaust. Everyone was talking about it; the massive slaughter of innocent humans. We prayed for these people in church services and privately. The mind-boggling massacre of Poland's scientists and journalists was being committed by Hitler's Nazi German henchmen in occupied Poland. A man named Karl Fritzsch was using a cyanide-based pesticide called Zyklon B, to execute prisoners of war from the Soviet Union en masse at Auschwitz Concentration Camp. I was familiar with this pesticide from my days as a chemist. I knew what it could do to insects, and was horrified it was being used on innocent people. The thought sickened me and made me unable to sleep many nights, as I thought about their agonizing deaths. As the new school year began, we heard of the requirement for Jewish people to wear the Star of David with the word "Jew" inscribed on it. The mandate was for all Jews, even schoolchildren in German-occupied areas. My heart was heavy. I knew my Lord Jesus was Jewish.

In spite of the dreadful war overseas and the somewhat depressed economy we were still dealing with, the school year was going smoothly. My students and I settled into a happy routine. The FFA and vocational agriculture classes were very popular. I had full classes each period and was comfortable in my role as an educator. I knew this was where God had placed me. I worked hard, as though I was working for Him.

When I went to Green Ridge, the previous agriculture teacher did not consult with the Missouri University Agricultural Extension agent, in Pettis County. The two men did not communicate or work together. I felt it made sense to unify our efforts. If we would combine our knowledge and resources, it would benefit the vocational agriculture students and the community. I began to work with the extension agent to accomplish our mutual goals. We got along very well. Our professional relationship helped others realize that with a little effort, our programs could benefit everyone.

Nita and I discussed marriage. Although I had dated other ladies in college and after college, I had never discussed marriage with anyone. My ideas about marriage were influenced by my parents' marriage. They were polite, kind and gentle with each other. I heard my father say they had never had an argument even though they worked side-by-side every day of their lives. I realized that this kind of relationship was a treasure. To have a marriage like theirs was the desire of my heart. Nita and I were excited and secretly planned to marry in December, during my Christmas break from school.

One quiet Sunday morning, on December 7th, I was going about my day as usual, when suddenly I heard church bells and sirens. Everyone turned on their radios and began listening to terrible news. Incredibly, the United States was attacked by the Japanese at Pearl Harbor in Hawaii. More than 2,400 American servicemen were killed that day. The surprise attack was a profound shock to everyone. I drove to Sedalia to see Nita. She was frightened. We could not guess what the future held for anyone. Over coffee that afternoon, we decided it seemed wise to wait a little longer to get married. I could be drafted into service for our country at any moment. We were warned the United States could be attacked again at any time. Nita and I discussed what she should do if we were attacked again.

The next day, our nation entered World War II when the United States declared war on Japan. Canada soon followed our lead in declaring war on Japan. No one could think about anything but the war and national safety.

For the remaining classes in December, I led discussions on current events and how those events were changing our world. The teenagers had very strong emotions ranging from indignation to anger and fear. All of them wanted to do something to help our country. It was patriotism, pure and simple, in every heart. The students asked hard questions. If I did not know the answers to their questions, we would search for answers together. I brought newspapers to class. We anxiously watched the prices of stocks and agricultural commodities. The young people were concerned that we would again be thrown into a severe depression. We were all fearful we might be bombed like Pearl Harbor had been. Some of the young men were angry and ready to enlist in service for our country. They wanted to fight back. Others wanted to wait to see if they got drafted. I knew after Christmas break, I would have smaller classes in high school and in the Young Farmers Group. My objective was to help them make wise decisions about their futures.

On Christmas Eve, I took Nita to my parents' home. She was nervous about meeting my large family. Everyone tried to make her feel welcome. She was timid, and self-conscious, but smiled often. I took her to see the places that were important in my life; Bethel Church, Grandma Shirley's house, Hickory Grove School and Princeton High School. That Christmas I gave Nita a gold cameo ring. On the way back to Sedalia, we again discussed marriage. We still felt we should wait to see if I was going to be drafted into service.

Nita and I knew her parents were financially unable to provide a wedding. Like my own parents, the Wharton family struggled to pay bills through the Depression years. We really did not want a large wedding, so we came up with a plan we felt was best for us. The only question was when would be the best time to get married.

After Christmas, life began to change rapidly. The nation geared up for war and the defense of our nation. Many young men enlisted in all branches of the service. In the following weeks, over half of the young men in my Young Farmers Group were drafted. One good result from this was the unemployment rate went down to 4.7 percent. That was the lowest in my memory.

The government began rationing food, gas, tires and even clothing. We were asked to conserve on everything. My mind kept going back to the hard Depression years. I vividly remembered not having what I needed to live from day to day. We now had a little more money, but were not allowed to buy necessities. We were all greatly affected by rationing. Rationing was supposed to reduce public anger about shortages. People on any income level could purchase a little of what was available. It seemed many people were quite upset at the government's involvement in their daily lives. After the initial adjustment, most people dealt quietly with the shortages, and understood it was our patriotic duty as we pressed toward a common goal. I think by this time we all had considered how drastically our lives would change if we lost this war. As sons and daughters of the Depression, we were already very frugal. We knew how to sacrifice without complaint and make do with what we had.

My superintendent came to see me and asked if I was registered for the draft. Of course I was. I had registered, as required, in East St. Louis, Illinois. He informed me he planned to write to my draft board and explain there was no way I could be replaced and he was requesting a deferment for me. Soon the draft board responded to him, saying they understood the situation and I would not be called into service. His statement was accurate. There were no vocational agriculture teachers available. In fact, all teachers were in short supply at the time.

Virginia moved to Kansas City, hoping to find a better paying job. Many industries were hiring due to the war effort. She got a job working in a munitions plant. Nita was very stretched financially, trying to pay for the little apartment by herself, but we hoped it might not be long before we married.

One day, Nita borrowed a dime from me. I had no intentions of asking her to pay it back. She was not in agreement with that and tried to repay me several times. Shortly after that, while we were driving in my car, Nita handed me a dime, and again I refused it. I wanted to bless her and help her get by. She was insistent, so I took the dime and threw it out the car window. I will never forget the aghast look on her face. She had earned the dime by washing and pin curling hair for ladies. Through the years, we laughed about this incident.

On Valentine's Day, I surprised Nita with a big card, a box of Whitman's chocolate candies and a heart-shaped gold locket. I had learned my sweetheart loved sweets and chocolate. She set a framed picture of us on a tree stump, and took a picture of the picture. When she developed the film, she cut out our heads and put them into her new locket. They were the perfect size.

Mr. and Mrs. Raymond D. Hagan on their wedding day

Schools in Green Ridge were called off on Friday, March 7th. I got up early and drove to Sedalia to pick up Nita. Together we drove to Kansas City and picked up Virginia and Nita's cousin, Richard Carr, who lived near Virginia. Then we went to the courthouse in Liberty to get a marriage license. At the parsonage of a Methodist minister, Rev. McKee, Valetta Juanita Wharton and I were quietly married on March 7, 1942, in Liberty, Missouri. Juanita wore a light blue dress, with matching accessories and a corsage of pink carnations that I bought for her. Virginia stood up for us, wearing a rose pink suit and a corsage of white carnations with pink edges. Richard Carr of Kansas City, Kansas, served as my best man. We had our picture taken immediately after the wedding. When the photographer said, "Mrs. Hagan, tilt your head just a bit," I was caught off guard and looked around for my mother. I did not realize that Nita was now Mrs. Hagan. We all laughed.

After the photographs were taken, all four of us went out to eat in downtown Kansas City. I rented three rooms at the famous Muehlebach Hotel. The following day, we went sightseeing in downtown Kansas City. I could not help thinking about the first time I was in Kansas City, arriving on the back of a load of cattle. I had to laugh at myself, thinking what lengths I had gone to in order to attend the American Royal and the National FFA Convention. It seemed almost like a dream from a hundred years past.

That evening, Nita and I returned to Sedalia as Mr. and Mrs. Raymond Hagan. As the minister had quoted from Genesis 2:24, we were no longer two, but one flesh. We had joined our union with Christ as the head of our marriage. I also remembered the scripture in Ecclesiastes 4:11 that said, "A cord of three strands is not quickly broken." It was comforting to realize in these times of uncertainty, I was not carrying the load alone. I had divine assistance.

We had not told anyone, except our families, about our wedding. We were still living separately, because we had no place to live together in Green Ridge. In that tiny community, apartments were nearly impossible to find. We would see each other an hour or two at night, but decided this could not go on. When we got our wedding photographs from Liberty, Missouri, we put our wedding announcement and a photograph in the Sunday edition of the Sedalia paper. We decided this was a great way to share our good news. I spoke to the superintendent of schools to tell him I had gotten married. He lived in a house that was divided into two apartments. Nita and I were able to rent the other apartment for $10.35 a month. When the article came out in the paper, I told my parents we had found a place to rent together. It was partially furnished, but not adequately. It had a small kitchen and living room downstairs and one bedroom upstairs. There was an old metal bed in the bedroom, but it was not assembled. Nita and I struggled to put the bed together, straightened up the kitchen, and had dinner. It began to feel more like a home. We were exhausted and soon fell asleep. In the middle of the night, the bed fell apart. The floor did not have a rug, so it sounded like the house was hit by a bomb. We tried, but were unable to get the bed back together. We attempted to sleep on the mattress on the floor. We could not stop laughing, as we imagined what my superintendent and his wife must be thinking. The next day he asked me about the noise. I told him the bed had broken. He never stopped heckling me about that incident.

Nita and I realized my students and friends might try to chivaree us. This was a common practice and viewed as a harmless joke to play on newlyweds. Friends and neighbors would arrive when they thought the newlyweds were asleep, and begin making a huge racket. The goal was to wake up the couple in the middle of the night and come into their home. The tradition in our neighborhood was, the chivareeers would not leave until they had been fed some type of snacks. We had refreshments available just in case we had midnight guests. Several weeks went by, so we forgot about it and ate the snacks.

At eleven-thirty one nght, Nita and I were sound asleep. Suddenly, we were awakened by a terrible noise. People were yelling and beating on pots and pans and running spoons up and down washboards. What a racket! I ran downstairs to shut the kitchen window we had left open. Too late. One of my students was already halfway into the house. As soon as his feet hit the floor, I ordered him to get out fast. He couldn't find the door, so I pointed and he ran out. I locked it behind him and then locked the window. By this time, Nita was dressed. We opened the doors and let them come in, so they would stop the terrible noisemaking. We really did not have enough food to feed them all. A neighbor signaled me from our back door. I went over and she gave me a large bag of candy to pass out. I was very grateful. Nita made popcorn, coffee and tea. We all laughed and had a good visit. I must say, we were relieved when they left.

As the end of the school year approached, I was feeling conviction. Nearly all of the Young Farmers Group had been called for service in the United States military. The minimum draft age was lowered from twenty-one to eighteen. Many of my vocational agriculture students were leaving high school, and then enlisting with parental permissions. This was a time in history when patriotism, loyalty and honor meant everything. I determined to finish teaching the school year to fulfill my obligation, and then enlist to proudly serve my nation.

Chapter 20

I'M IN THE ARMY NOW!
ARMY AIR FORCE THAT IS....

At the end of March, in 1942, I tried to enlist in the Navy Air Corps. Unfortunately, I failed the physical due to the condition of my nose. As a young student at Hickory Grove School, I had completely shattered my nose. I was still unable to breathe normally through my nose, and experienced frequent nose bleeds. I was disheartened. But I was not ready to give up.

In April, I saw an advertisement in the Sedalia newspaper that said instructors were needed to train pilots. A program was starting soon to train the needed instructors. In June of 1941, United States Army Air Corps became the Army Air Forces. This new branch of our military was training the flight instructors. I was excited about this possibility. The more I considered it, the more I realized it was a good fit for me. I could utilize my teaching skills to help my country in their time of need. I had always had a keen interest in flying.

Prior to 1940, the United States Army had few pilots, and even fewer airplanes. As war seemed more likely, the number of pilots grew rapidly from 982 in 1939, to approximately 8,000 in 1940, and over 27,000 in 1941. Even with these record numbers, many more pilots were still needed. At that time, the United States Army Air Corps could not sufficiently handle training the large number of flying cadets required. The U.S. Army Air Forces relied on additional pilots from the CPTP (Civilian Pilot Training Program) and a large network of civilian flight schools under contract to the U.S. Army Air Corps, as well as conducting training in its own schools. Between 1939 and 1945, the CPTP would train more than 435,000 pilots, logging an incredible 12 million flight hours.

I'm in the army now! Army Air Force that is....

As soon as school was out in May of 1942, I resigned my teaching position at Green Ridge and enlisted in the United States Army Air Forces, specifically as a flight instructor. Many people were trying to get in this program. In just two weeks I found out that I had been accepted into the program.

I was ordered to report to an area near Knob Noster, Missouri. I was given the choice to stay in a temporary barracks, or find a place of my own. I found a furnished apartment in nearby Warrensburg, Missouri, and rented it for Nita and me. The rent was nine dollars per month. I was in the Army Air Forces flight training course. I was required to pass written tests immediately. I took the first tests in Kansas City. I was able to pass and was sent to the Knob Noster area to begin the training course. There were twenty men in my class. We took classes to learn about flying, various planes, engines, and how to read the instruments. There were over fifty schools like ours in operation around the United States. After completing the course, we would be sent across the nation to train pilots. My class flew out of the little airport in Warrensburg, Missouri, just nine miles from Knob Noster. The flight classes were intense, running early in the morning until late at night. They trained us as fast as possible. The instructors traded off teaching almost in a tag team style. I studied constantly in the few hours we had as free time.

We learned about many kinds of planes and what we could do with each of them. We also learned about flight theory. Pre-Flight stage coursework taught

The first plane I flew.

the mechanics and physics of flight and required the cadets to pass courses in mathematics and science. Then we were taught to apply our knowledge practically by learning about aeronautics and thinking in three dimensions. I was focused, trying to retain massive quantities of information. Only after passing the coursework were we able to begin the actual flight training. The first time I went up in a plane, I went with an instructor. It was one-on-one training. He flew and I observed. I did this two or three times each day, then went back to class. Most of the cadets sat and waited for an instructor to ask them to go up. They were observers in planes only once a day. Any time I saw an instructor, I would ask him to go up with me. Before long, I was flying and the instructor was beside me. Flying a plane was exhilarating. The absolute joy I felt when flying a plane was unmatched.

Primary Pilot Training taught basic flight using two-seater aircraft. The most popular primary trainer planes were the Stearman PT-13 and PT-17 "Kaydet," the Fairchild PT-19 "Cornell," and the Ryan PT-20 "Recruit."

The flight portion of the course was three months long. By the end of the first month, I flew by myself. Most other cadets were not yet flying alone. The first few times I flew alone were scary. We had to watch carefully to see if we were clear to take off, or land, as there were no air traffic controllers at the Warrensburg Sky Haven Airport. However, we were the only ones using the airport. We flew two kinds of planes. On my first few flights, I flew a PT-19, a single engine, two-seater plane. We flew in daytime only during this part of the training. We were required to keep flight logbooks and a pilot information file supplied by the Army Air Forces. I kept flying alone as much as possible. My in-flight hours added up quickly. I was resolved to finish each assignment to the best of my abilities.

We performed various training maneuvers, such as a spin, pulling out of a spin, and rollovers. Soon I was able to do it by myself. One day after I did a spin and pulled out, my engine stalled. I was just floating. Trying not to panic, I began to look for a place to land, but all I saw were trees and hills. I had the nose of the plane pointed slightly down to keep moving. Remembering a class lesson I tried pointing the nose of the plane straight down. Thankfully the wind resistance caused the propeller to start turning again. What a great relief. I immediately went back to the airstrip. I felt weak in the knees and could hardly get out of the cockpit and walk. The instructor asked, "What in the world is wrong with you?" I leaned on the plane as I explained that the engine stalled out, but I was able to restart it by pointing the nose straight down. The instructor was openly skeptical and hatefully said that it did not happen. He told me to get back in the plane. I went around to the passenger side and he took off down the runway at full throttle. I was praying. All at once the engine died. He went completely off the runway, to the fence, turning in circles before he could stop the plane. He got out cussing at the plane, but now believed my story. We had learned in class it was theoretically possible to start a stalled engine by pointing the nose straight down. Now we had proof. My angry instructor got it started again by pulling down on the propeller. Back at the hanger, he cussed out the mechanic and told him to get it fixed.

After a little over a month into the three-month course, the trainers said I had done everything I needed to do. I was elated.

Flight Instructors in Warrensburg, Missouri

They sent me to the second part of the training. Part two was held in Kansas City, Missouri. Once again, Nita and I moved close to my training location. We were able to find an upstairs apartment, in an old red brick house in Kansas City. It was conveniently located for me. Being a small-town girl, Nita was uncomfortable with her safety in the city neighborhood. She rarely went out of the apartment without me.

Our training site was the downtown Kansas City municipal airport. It is located near the Missouri River. I was in a class of twenty cadets. They were from all over the country and had finished the first course just as I had done. Instructors gave lectures covering various types of airplanes and safety procedures. The planes that I flew in Kansas City were bigger, heavier, and faster.

These planes could do more than the little prop planes we had flown in the first course. Basic Pilot Training also taught cadets to fly in formation, by instruments or aerial navigation, at night, and for longer distances. We flew various aircraft such as the Vultee BT-13 "Valiant," and we were exactingly evaluated. One day as I was landing my plane, I saw a large passenger plane coming into the same runway for a landing. I was almost down so I had to think quickly. I landed my plane in the grass beside the runway, next to the large passenger plane. That was too close for comfort. My heart was racing. I was given recognition for quick thinking and a good landing.

Nita in front of our apartment in Kansas City

Nita and I celebrated our first Christmas as a married couple in December of 1942. We were very poor and barely able to pay our bills, but we were happy to be together. We kept my bank account in Green Ridge, Missouri. I sent my meager paycheck there each month. The stamp cost three cents. Sometimes we struggled to buy groceries for dinner. To help us keep on a strict budget, we recorded everything we spent in a journal. Our rent was twenty-five dollars a month for a small, one-bedroom furnished apartment. This included water and electricity. One special evening we saw the movie "Holiday Inn." We both loved the song Bing Crosby sang, called "White Christmas." This was a holiday splurge for us. We desperately needed tires for our car, but it was nearly impossible to obtain tires, due to the wartime mandates. Rubber was needed for the military. When tires did become available, they were outrageously expensive. We had no other choice, so we patched the tires and kept using them. Since gas was also rationed, we were unable to visit my family this Christmas. The ration coupons had expiration dates, so it was difficult to save them ahead for trips. We were able to save enough gas coupons to go to LaMonte, Missouri to see Nita's parents on Christmas Day. Nita's mother, Valetta Wharton, prepared a wonderful feast. It was the best food we had eaten in a long time. She even sent leftovers home with us. We felt very blessed.

    The day after Christmas, we began a more difficult aspect of our flight training. For this, we used an area near the Missouri river just outside of Kansas City. It had rough terrain, a very short runway and was difficult to locate as it was hidden from view, until we were directly above it. It was little more than a small field. These difficulties were what we were learning to handle. We would only use this area for flight maneuvers. This was important, as military pilots need to adapt to difficult surroundings.

    One evening in 1943 we had a huge snowstorm. The snow was wet and heavy. Over a foot of snow fell overnight. The next morning, I could hardly get my car to the airport on my treadless tires. I asked the instructor if we were supposed to fly. He said to take the plane up and practice landing at the river bottom training area. It was difficult to tell where the landing strip was in the deep snow. When I landed, the snow stopped me quickly. I could not get enough speed through the snow to get back up in the air. I had to come up with a plan. I decided to taxi my plane back and forth to pack down a spot long enough to attempt a takeoff. I got just enough speed to clear the fence and get up in the air. I returned to the Kansas City municipal airport and landed. The instructor was angry with me and asked why I was back so soon. While he was still yelling, another instructor joined the conversation and told us that due to the weather, no flying was allowed. I was the only trainee to fly that day. I soon passed level two of my flight training and was sent on to level three. I was the only one in my class to pass level two at that time. I also had nearly twice as many in-flight hours logged in my record book as the other students. Without any doubt I was successful because I was unwavering in my determination to do my very best for our country.

    The third and final part of training was held at Des Moines, Iowa. Once again, Nita and I moved. It was springtime of 1943. This time we found a lower level apartment in a good neighborhood. The furnished apartment was rented by the week for seven dollars. This was a little more than the upstairs apartment, but it was important because Nita was expecting our first child, making stairs a difficulty. We were both excited. We considered names for boys and girls. Nita seemed to be feeling well. Due to memories of my older sister Jessie dying in childbirth, I made sure Nita got excellent medical care.

The training area in Des Moines had been a commercial airport and was well maintained. The airport was not used commercially during the war. For the advanced pilot training we flew the most powerful and biggest planes we had encountered. This was also the best training course. We flew greater distances and did advanced maneuvers. The instructors would give us a destination, Rockford, Illinois, for example, and we would have to plot a flight plan. We were trained to fly and land in the dark. Sometimes planes were wrecked doing this. It was not easy, but I never crashed.

My nose bled every time I went up in a plane. I had not told the instructors. Instead, I would manage by stuffing my nose with cotton balls. I knew this was caused by the broken nose I received while trying to move a big rock in the schoolyard when I was a child.

One evening it was sleeting and raining when I came in for a landing. I saw a burning plane on the landing strip. With my heart beating fast, I watched the plane in front of me land and try to avoid the burning plane and fire trucks. He slid off the icy runway. Realizing my fuel was getting low, I knew I had to land somewhere very quickly. I decided to go beyond both planes, landing on the other side of them. It was a risky idea. I was able to land, but did not have much runway left. I had to spin the plane around to stop. In spite of the ice and the very short area available, I was able to land safely and maintain control of my plane. I was given recognition for that landing.

Level Three cadets were taught to do air acrobatics, as fighter pilots would do if they were under attack. This included loops to reverse direction, rollovers to both sides, and also front to back rollovers. I enjoyed doing the air acrobatics more than anything I had ever done. I tried to practice these maneuvers at every opportunity. My flight log showed more hours in the air than any other cadet in this course as well.

I finished first in all three classes. After the completion of the third course, the Army Air Force sent men to give flying and written tests. Part of the written test was to identify various airport locations in faraway places on maps. I was the first one finished with the comprehensive testing by two weeks. I was ecstatic the day I was certified as a flight instructor. I had worked hard to complete my goal and was looking forward to serving my country as long as they needed me. But I had to pass another physical.

The Army sent a gruff, older military doctor to give my physical. He examined me carefully. I had passed the physical with flying colors so far. After putting me through every kind of test imaginable, he roughly stuck an instrument up my nose to look inside. Blood poured out of my nose. He would not pass me because of my bad nose. I tried to talk him into passing me. He refused, saying

Army Air Corps ★ 1942 - 1943

STUDENT PILOT CERTIFICATE NO. S336691

UNITED STATES OF AMERICA
DEPARTMENT OF COMMERCE
CIVIL AERONAUTICS ADMINISTRATION
WASHINGTON

Form 340 ACA, Rev. 8-1-40
PASSENGER CARRYING PROHIBITED

THIS CERTIFICATE MUST BE CARRIED AT ALL TIMES WHILE PILOTING AIRCRAFT

This certifies that Raymond Dale Hagan is properly qualified and is physically able to perform the duties of a Student Pilot.

Address: Green Ridge Mo.

DATE OF BIRTH	WEIGHT	HEIGHT	HAIR	EYES	SEX
4-5-15	117	5'4½"	Bl	Br	M

The holder hereof is now physically qualified for no higher grade of pilot certificate than that of Commercial-Army

Date of Issuance: 8-25-42

Signature of Student Pilot: Raymond D Hagan

CERTIFICATED INSTRUCTOR'S ENDORSEMENTS

This certifies that the holder has complied with the Civil Air Regulations and, in my opinion, is competent to make a First Solo Flight under my supervision.

Date: Sept 30/42 — Signature of Instructor: James William Rustin

DATE	TYPE	LAND OR WATER	Wt. & Engine	SIGNATURE OF INSTRUCTOR AND CERTIFICATE NO.
	Inverted		0-40	James William Rustin 331-40
Dec 3/42	Howard DG-A Land		80-165	Ray H Baker 39787
3/12/43	Interstate Land		10-115	Richard Kemp C-695-40

This certifies that the holder has complied with the Civil Air Regulations and, in my opinion, is competent to make a First Solo Cross Country Flight under my supervision.

IDENTIFICATION CARD—ENLISTED RESERVE CORPS

This is to Certify, That Raymond D. Hagan Pvt. Air Force, Serial No. 17115752, Home address Mercer, Missouri, was enlisted in grade shown in Air Force Enlisted Reserve Corps of the Army of the United States, on the 27th day of August, one thousand nine hundred and forty-two, for the period of DOW & 6 mos when he was 27 years of age, and by occupation a School Teacher. He has brown eyes, brown hair, ruddy complexion, and is 5 feet 4½ inches in height.

Dates of immunization: Smallpox _____ Typhoid _____ Other _____ Blood type _____

Given at Headquarters Kansas Recruiting District this 27th day of August, one thousand nine hundred and forty-two.

FOR THE COMMANDING OFFICER: H. C. Heald

it was the worst nose he had seen. I was overwhelmed. I could not believe I would not be allowed to train pilots, or even to fly. I was stunned.

The Army gave me papers to fill out with two choices. I could choose to take an honorable discharge or go into the grounds crew. I was honestly heartbroken. The life and career I desired so desperately suddenly vanished.

I chose grounds crew and put the letter in the mailbox at the corner of my street. I wished Nita was there by my side, but due to my long working hours and being late in her pregnancy, she was staying with my parents on the family farm. I sadly went back to the airport and flew an airplane almost all night. I landed the plane for the last time, and walked slowly to my car. That night when I finally got into bed, I started thinking and praying about my decision. I changed my mind. I decided I could do more to help our country as a teacher than I could as part of a grounds crew.

I immediately got up and went to the corner to stand by the mailbox, waiting for the mailman to come. It seemed like a long wait as I stood there praying, but at last he arrived. I explained my situation to him, and even described the envelope. I asked him for my letter back, but he insisted he could not do that. He opened the box and my letter was lying on top. He hesitated and then said, "Take it, but don't ever tell anyone." He turned his back and I snatched my letter. I ran back to the apartment, tore open the letter and changed it from grounds crew to honorable discharge and mailed it the second time. I called Nita and told her our future was changing again. I was given an honorable discharge, officially, on July 15, 1943, after just fourteen months in the Army Air Force.

I packed our belongings, got in my car and drove home to the Hagan family farm. Nita and my parents were waiting for me. They realized I was overwhelmingly disappointed, and gave me a warm welcome home. There on the peaceful farm, I poured my heart out to God, praying for redirection, and to know His exact will for my life. The beautiful farm and the comfort of my loving family soothed my spirit. The Lord again answered my prayers, and we were certain of the path we were to follow. Nita and I stayed with my parents briefly until we could begin the next stage of our lives. I knew with the Lord ordering my steps the best was yet to be.

Psalm 32:8
"I will instruct you and teach you in the way you should go;
I will counsel you with my loving eye on you."

Army of the United States

Honorable Discharge

This is to certify that

PRIVATE   HAGAN, RAYMOND D.   AFER (CPT)

17115757

Army of the United States

is hereby Honorably Discharged from the military service of the United States of America.

This certificate is awarded as a testimonial of Honest and Faithful Service to his country.

Given at   OMAHA, NEBRASKA

Date   15 July 1943

EDW. P. NOYES
Colonel CAC

W. D., A. G. O. Form No. 55
January 22, 1943

Chapter 21

THE REST OF MY STORY

The rest of my story is not an ending, but a beginning. When I died as a young college student, I told the Lord I had not done much in my life. He graciously allowed me to return from the spirit realm. This amazing blessing has often been in my thoughts. I hope that my life has pleased Him. My choices and decisions have been made with prayer and contemplation. He instilled in me a desire to help and encourage others; to place their needs before my own.

Just as planets rotate around the sun, my life rotates in a circle of interaction with the Future Farmers of America and the amazing field of Vocational Agriculture. There is no doubt in my mind this is the career path I was supposed to follow. After a year teaching vocational agriculture in Cainesville, Missouri, Mr. G.K. Arney, my high school vocational agriculture teacher from Princeton, Missouri, chose me to take his place when he retired. Nita and I moved to Princeton with our first baby daughter, named after her mother, Sharon Juanita. What fun and what a blessing to be in the halls of Princeton High School once more. I was excited to be able to give blessings back to the wonderful community and people of Princeton, Missouri. I felt I was hitting my stride as a teacher. I knew I was meant to teach. I poured endless energy and excitement into my classes and the FFA.

At the end of my second year at Princeton High School, in spring of 1946, three of my students were awarded the State Farmers Degree at the state FFA convention held in Columbia, Missouri. This is the highest state level FFA degree. The students awarded this degree were Harvey Wright, Jr., Winston Oswalt, and Wendell Moore. At the time, Mercer County was the only county in the state to have three young men receive the degree. The State Farmer Degree is awarded on projects, scholarship, leadership, and a test given by state FFA officials.

The next several years held new opportunities to mentor other fine young men like Herbert Covey as he earned the American Farmer Degree. This is the highest FFA degree awarded on the national level. In 1947, Lester Slayton, Jr., earned the Missouri State Farmer Degree. 1948 was a record-breaking year for Princeton High School when four of our young men earned the Missouri State Farmer Degree. I was proud of my students. The four young men were Bobby Stinson, Danny Gentry, Wayne Hughes and Bill Michael. I made lifelong friends among these good people.

Princeton High School FFA. Ray Hagan seated on the front row, right end

While I was working and raising a family, many changes were taking place on the Hagan farm. In December of 1946, Raycel realized his lifelong dream and bought the Hagan Family Farm from Mom and Dad. Raycel, Ruby and their children moved into the original house on the farm. What a wonderful family legacy to live and work on the same farm as our father, Ross, and Great-uncle Jake before him.

Public Sale

As we have sold our farm and are moving we will sell at the farm located 14 miles north of Princeton, 10 miles west of Mercer, 6 miles southeast of Pleasanton, on gravel road, on

TUESDAY, NOV. 12

Beginning at 11 O'Clock, the following: *1947*

49   HEAD OF LIVESTOCK   49

CATTLE

Fifteen head of registered Herefords, consisting of 5 cows, ranging in age from 3 to 5 years, good ones; 3 yearling heifers; 4 heifer calves; two bull calves and one herd bull to be 2 years old in April, a good one. These cattle are Domino breeding.

DAIRY CATTLE

Jersey cow, 7 years old, giving milk now, will be fresh in February; cow 6 years old, half Holstein and half Jersey, will be fresh Dec. 1; Jersey cow, will be 3 years old in spring, to be fresh in November; Jersey cow and calf; two half Jersey yearling heifers; Jersey yearling heifer to be fresh about April 1; red yearling heifer, to bring calf in spring; and black Whiteface calf

6   HEAD OF HORSES   6

Bay horse, smooth mouth, weight 1350; grey mare, smooth mouth, weight 1100; black horse, 11 years old, weight 1100; black horse, 8 years old, weight 1100; black saddle mare, smooth mouth; bay saddle mare, smooth mouth.

HOGS

Around 12 head of registered Spotted Poland China boars and gilts. All eligible for registry. All top breeding and good farm-type hogs.

FARM IMPLEMENTS

Iron wheel wagon, good as new; iron wheel wagon with new hay rack; car wagon with box; John Deere corn planter with wire; McCormick mowing machine, 6-ft., Emerson mowing machine, 6-ft.; sulky rake, 10-ft.; wheat drill, 6-ft.; disk, 7-ft.; 15-ft. harrow; 10-ft. harrow; 8-ft. harrow; spring tooth cultivator; 16-in breaking plow; 14-in breaking plow; 5-shovel garden plow; single shovel plow; endgate oats seeder; tight wagon box, a good one; hay track for barn, 30 ft long, complete with fork; set of 1¾ in. harness, good ones; set of chain tug harness; saddle; horse collars; corn sheller wheelbarrow; spring wagon; 3 new hog houses, 6 x 8 ft.; some lumber, including 2 x 8-14ft.; 2 x 6-14-ft. and other lengths; laths; house doors, windows; screen doors, etc., and about 700 brick; hog oiler; bee gums; cross cut saw; 2 axes; post auger; hay knife; pitchforks; dinner bell; 2 scoop endgates; 4-horse doubletree; 3-horse doubletree; wagon doubletree; wagon neck yokes; a few posts; lawnmower; 8 or 9 gal. of barn paint; other things too numerous to mention.

HOUSEHOLD GOODS

Majestic range with warming closet and reservoir; oil stove with built-in oven, used only one year; 13-in. Round Oak heating stove; kitchen cabinet; dining room table; 3 beds; 3 sets of springs; mattress; chairs; rocking chairs; chiffoneer; 2 dressers, stand table; music cabinet; phonograph with records; Minnesota model A sewing machine; 2 Alladin lamps; gasoline lamp; new electric iron; 2 gasoline irons; 2 sets sad irons; good electric cream separator, or can be turned by hand; one power plant motor

Terms—Nothing to be removed until settled for.

ROSS HAGAN

Col. Tom Jones, Auct.   Allen Brown, Clerk

Lunch By Bethel Ladies Club

The rest of my story

In 1947, my parents moved to a small retirement farm near Trenton, Missouri. Mom, Dad, and all of our family were proud of Raycel and Ruby for continuing the tradition of successful farming on the family farm. It was difficult for my parents to leave the only home and community they had ever known. It was especially hard for Mom. She had never been away from her sister, Gertrude or Bethel Church. Although it is almost unheard of today, both of my parents lived their entire lives a few miles from their birthplace, until they retired. My parents greatly missed worshipping with friends and family at Bethel Church. Sometimes they would return to visit on Sunday and then have dinner with family. After the move, I saw my mother shed quiet tears of homesickness. In time, she was able to overcome her sadness and make a new home. Again Dad planted an orchard; Mom raised chickens and planted rows of peonies along their driveway. They continued to garden, raise bees, dairy cows, and sheep. This small retirement farm was only twenty acres.

Dad utilized his excellent carpentry skills to build several houses. They purchased a few rental houses in Trenton. For this hardworking couple, retirement meant slowing down but not stopping work. They attended church in Trenton. Mom joined a ladies circle class, making new friends. I have great love and respect for the family God placed me in.

As World War II ended, I started a Farm Veterans Program in the evenings. Working two full-time jobs was hectic, but I loved the challenge. This program quickly became popular and the classes filled to capacity. Men who joined the military during WWII left as teenagers and came home as war-weary adults. As a way of saying 'thank you," Congress enacted what became known as the G.I. Bill of Rights. At the time, it was called the "Servicemen's Readjustment Act," signed by President Franklin D. Roosevelt in 1944. The Act gave servicemen returning from the war several benefits, including education and training, and loans for homes, farms, or businesses. Education was the most important part of the act. Veterans made up an incredible 49 percent of students enrolled in college in 1947. Some veterans never returned to the farms they left as teenagers. Others used the G.I. Bill of Rights to attend agriculture classes to become educated about the new technologies in farming.

It was an honor to start and implement Missouri's first program designed to help our veterans rejoin society and make wise career decisions. My successful veterans' programs caught the eye of the men in the State Department of Education, and I was asked to join their staff. I was offered a position with the Missouri Department of Elementary and Secondary Education as an area supervisor in the Vocational Agriculture Department.

After a great deal of prayer, and discussion with Nita, I was convinced this was an opportunity provided by the Lord. In January of 1948, I turned in my resignation to the Princeton School District and started working for the State Department of Education as an area supervisor. In May, Nita and I welcomed another blue-eyed baby girl into our family, little Jane Marie. She was named after my sister Vee Marie.

I was thankful I had prayed and followed God's direction to take the job with the State Department of Education. I loved my new position so much I stayed for thirty-six years. Nita and our growing family of girls moved first to Warrensburg and then to Jefferson City, Missouri. I became more involved when I accepted the additional responsibility as State FFA Executive Secretary. My life was busy and happy. I truly enjoyed running the annual state FFA Convention each spring. At that time, I did not realize I would remain involved with this convention for the next sixty-five years.

It was an honor to help with the National FFA Convention in Kansas City every fall. I had loved this convention since the first time I attended as a poor high school teenager, without money, transportation or a place to stay. Now I attended and helped with the planning and implementation of these conventions every year through the turn of the century and forward, until it was moved to another state.

The American Royal in Kansas City, Missouri, is a livestock show, horse show and rodeo held each year in October and November at the Kemper Arena.

Ray Hagan

The Future Farmers of America was founded during the American Royal. Kansas City's professional baseball team, the Kansas City Royals, derive their name from the American Royal. The American Royal has one of the Midwest's largest livestock exhibitions, with separate youth divisions for 4-H and FFA. I served as Assistant Superintendent of the FFA department of the American Royal livestock and horse show for thirty years. As part of this role, I began coordinating the FFA Division of the livestock show. This required careful planning with the American Royal staff and the FFA chapters around the state. Through the years, I worked with thousands of FFA youth showing their sheep, cattle and swine. The hay bales stacked between the pens was a constant reminder of a poor, hungry, Depression era country boy who gratefully slept on the hay bales.

Even though I was busy, I felt I needed to earn a master's degree to be assured of continued employment and keep my skills sharp. I began to take classes in my spare time at the University of Missouri. This was a busy time for me as my job was very fast-paced. I received a master's degree in education, from the University of Missouri in Columbia in 1951. This was an exciting day in my life.

Soon Nita and I were blessed with a third daughter, Janice Elaine. When she began to walk, we moved to Jefferson City and purchased our first home for $15,000. We were happy living in a larger community with our daughters. We joined a church and attended every week.

I began to consider getting a doctorate degree. When my older brother, Albert earned a doctorate degree, many opportunities became available to advance in his career. Albert received his doctorate in agriculture from Michigan State University. With his encouragement, in 1958 I took a sabbatical from work and pursued doctoral studies at Michigan State University. Nita and I moved our family to East Lansing, Michigan. We were able to find a nice apartment to rent. I enjoyed the course work and getting to know the differences between this university and the University of Missouri. My family also enjoyed a cooler climate. As I prayed for daily direction, I began to realize the Lord had planted me in the exact position He desired me to be. I knew this coursework was going to help me in my current position, but I also realized that after three years of absence, required to obtain this degree, my job would likely be filled by someone else. I moved Nita and our three young daughters back to Jefferson City, Missouri.

Shortly after we returned to Missouri, the State Department of Education asked me to take on an additional assignment to go along with my district supervisor duties

Nita and Ray on graduation day 1951
Master's degree in education

and the position as Executive Secretary of the Missouri FFA. I became Assistant Superintendent of the FFA Department of the Missouri State Fair. This involved careful planning, which began just after the fair was over each August and continued until the next August. The State Fair catalog was completed by January each year. "The Children's Barnyard" was a project I designed and developed to be run by FFA members. It allowed children to observe, touch and learn about various farm animals. This has been a favorite exhibit at the Missouri State Fair for many years. I also ran livestock judging contests for the FFA. I enjoyed watching youth "learn by doing" as they showed their livestock projects. I was fortunate to serve in this position for thirty years.

My love for the FFA caused me to write a book to provide a historical record of the development, growth, and achievement of the Missouri Future Farmers of America during its first fifty years. "FFA at 50 In Missouri" was a huge undertaking. Nita worked many nights helping me type the book. It is composed to a great extent of achievements of FFA members and chapters, in various state and national activities. To include the tremendous success stories of the thousands of FFA members through the years was beyond the framework of time and funds available for the book. I realized the strength of the FFA lies in the activities of individual chapters throughout the state, under the supervision of dedicated vocational agriculture instructors. Various activities at the chapter, area, state, and national levels provide the instructors and FFA officers the tools needed for motivation and achievement. This book provides a record of achievement during the first fifty years for many of these activities. It was completed in 1978 in time for the fiftieth birthday of the FFA in Missouri.

An important part of my position with the State Department included working directly with teachers on an individual basis. I delighted in visiting the vocational agriculture programs in all the schools in my district. I especially appreciated mentoring new teachers and watching them grow into leaders in their schools and community. We worked not only on teaching skills, but with their school boards in developing new curriculum ideas and new building plans.

Everyone has unique abilities and talents from the Lord. These differences make our lives distinctive and enable us to succeed in diverse areas. God has blessed me with discernment. He has used this to help me direct others into suitable areas of study and employment. The Lord also blessed me with a spirit of encouragement, which He has used to help others grow and reach their potential in life.

This was especially true when working with the State FFA officers' team each year. This team of carefully selected men and women dedicate a year or more of their life in high school or college to promote FFA programs. The officers speak at many public events, learning to refine their leadership and speaking

Ray Hagan, center front. Carl Humphrey is standing at the door.

skills. I spent endless hours with each team. These outstanding young people are the very best of our youth in the United States. Without exception, each one of these officers later became leaders in their chosen fields of employment and in their communities. What an honor it has been to watch these fine young men and women grow, becoming accomplished in many realms, including politics, law, education, business, television and broadcasting, and so much more. The list of 428 state officers I had the privilege to guide includes, in part: the late Congressman Jerry Litton; past director of agriculture James Boillot; Dr. Larry Case, past National Director of the FFA; Dr. Steve Brown, National FFA Advisor & Board Chairman National FFA Organization; and Dr. Terry Heiman, past Director of Vocational Agriculture in Missouri. It is a delight to see many of the FFA officers I mentored excel in their careers.

Whatever I do in life, it is important for me to do the task to the best of my ability. Quitting after encountering difficulties is simply not an option with me. Difficulties mean I need to find a different solution and remain focused on the goal. This is not about being a perfectionist or being unable to delegate responsibilities. Rather, it is a core philosophy of my life and upbringing. The following experience illustrates my attitude concerning life. One winter, B.W. Robinson, our Assistant Director at the State Department of Education, told all supervisors there was no money left in the budget for travel expenses. Our jobs were designed to travel extensively visiting schools to help teachers and work with the FFA. At the end of the following month, I turned in my expense account report to B.W. He called me in and said, "I told you that there is no money left for travel expenses." I told him I understood and I did not expect to get paid. I just wanted to do my job the best I could and that meant traveling. I felt I must travel to do my job well. He was surprised and pleased. There is a scripture that I learned as a child in Mom's Sunday school classes at Bethel Church:

Colossians 3:23 King James Bible (Cambridge Ed.)
And whatsoever ye do, do it heartily, as to the Lord, and not unto men;

My upbringing is very influential in the way I have met life's daily circumstances. Not only did I learn the practical truths in the Bible, but I saw daily role models to emulate. I give credit and glory for everything good in my life to my Lord Jesus.

I seemed to become one with my job and the FFA. I never considered my job to be work or drudgery. Never once did I wake up and think I'd rather not go to work. In fact, even when we went on vacation, I could not wait to get back to my life's work. I simply was happy doing a job that was fun and exciting every day. As I look back to the time I was living in East St. Louis, I remember listening to a man who worked for the railroad all his life. He was close to retirement. He sincerely hated his job and complained continuously. He taught me an excellent life lesson. What a blessing to be able to spend my life having fun and helping others to be their best.

I was involved with the FFA on the national level, serving as Superintendent of the National FFA livestock judging contest for six years and as Assistant Superintendent for twenty-four years. This required making frequent trips to Washington, D.C.

President Reagan saw the importance of vocational education and the FFA. Members of the National Council on Vocational Education recommended me to be on the President's committee for vocational agriculture. I was honored to accept this position. We helped direct the future of vocational education. The committee was responsible for advising the President on current needs in vocational education. President Reagan was pleased with the accomplishments of our committee.

My life has not been only about work. Nita and I were proud of our three fine daughters, Sharon, Jane and Janice.

I followed my parents' examples by raising my family in church and encouraging each one to get a good education. We took part in many activities with them and watched them grow into beautiful, hardworking women. I was proud

My daughters; Sharon, Janice and Jane

to become Papa Ray to two grandchildren, Patricia and Jeffrey; two great-grandchildren, LeeAnna and Austin; and three great-great-grandchildren, Chase, Sierra, and Gemma. The last time I saw my brother Raycel, he told me the most important thing in life is God, then family and the love they share. I agree. I will love my parents, siblings, children and grandchildren through all eternity.

Even with a wonderful family, considering retirement was difficult for me. But at the age of seventy, I knew I had to leave the world of vocational agriculture in the capable hands of a younger generation. So I left behind my position as State Executive Secretary of Missouri FFA on November 30, 1984. For forty-four years I had worked with thousands of FFA members in Missouri and watched them develop into successful life leaders. I would always be dedicated to the FFA. I would also miss being District Supervisor of Agricultural Education for the Department of Elementary and Secondary Education. But, after thirty-six years I knew I needed to find other outlets for my energies. The years I served in the field of vocational agriculture and the FFA were the happiest days of my life. The first six months of retirement I still worked regularly to help train the people new to our department. I worked to help them write the State Fair Catalog, and set up arrangements for the State FFA Convention and make the program. Steve Brown was chosen to take my position. He became an outstanding supervisor with integrity, wisdom and a vision for the future of our chosen field. By the time I retired, the directors on both the state and national levels were teachers and FFA officers I had mentored.

My family and I thought I might be unable to adjust to such a dramatic lifestyle change. Thankfully, it turned out the best days were still ahead. Life is full of unexpected surprises. A new lifestyle opened exciting possibilities in my life. It is simply perspective. God gives us exactly what we need for the season we are in. He supplies the talent, connections, resources, and experience we need for each moment. It doesn't mean that's all we are ever going to have. We may need more next month or next year. When that time comes, God will make sure that we have what we need. If we trust in the Lord, we don't have to worry. The Bible explains we lack no good thing if we follow Him and do His will.

Retirement has been filled with new experiences and people. A winter home in Arizona opened up possibilities for hiking, rock hound trips and dancing. Traveling the world with family has allowed me to experience firsthand the Lord's creativity. Nita and I owned and enjoyed two travel trailers.

Nita and Ray Hagan

After losing my lifelong companion when I was seventy-five, I had to learn how to live without Nita by my side. At first I thought my life was over. Slowly I remembered the Lord allowed me to return to life to live for Him. With prayer,

I was able to turn my focus away from my grief and focus on the Lord and other people once more. I recalled the example of my parents when they lost three family members in a few months. They had grieved but kept on living and doing what needed to be done each day. This is what I tried to do as well. I even tried painting to help me refocus and look forward rather than backward.

After a time, I met a wonderful lady who had a background similar to mine. We enjoyed dancing, traveling and hiking. Kay Kirtley and I were married and shared fourteen happy years together, residing in Arizona each winter, before she passed away.

Ray and Kay Hagan on their wedding day in 1992

In 2007, the Hagan Hereford Farm, which was established by my family in 1875, was presented with a Century Farm Award by the Mercer County Extension Office for being in one family for over 100 years. That came to 132 years on the day of the award. Sadly, my brother, Raycel did not live to see this. It was an honor for me to accept this award with my sister-in-law, Ruby and her sons, who are currently running the farm. The Century Farm Award is presented to those families who have contributed to local, state, national, and international agriculture by owning and operating the same Missouri farm for 100 years or more.

The beautiful and solid barn built by my father, Ross Hagan, was carefully maintained by my brother, Raycel and sister-in-law, Ruby. It still sits squarely on its foundation. The barn was the 2009 grand prize winner in a classic barn photo contest sponsored by <u>Living The Country Life</u> magazine. As grand prize winner, the Hagan barn was featured on the cover of the April 2010 issue of <u>Living the Country Life</u> magazine. I have always known it is the most beautiful barn in America. I am delighted others think so too. My sister-in-law, Ruby was also presented with a hand carved barn plaque, crafted by artisan Dorrel Harrison. My dad would be amazed to know his wonderful red barn is still a community landmark as it reaches its 100th birthday.

It has been a blessing to live in the warmth and sunshine of Arizona for twenty-eight winters. With careful scheduling, I have returned from Arizona in time to attend the Missouri State FFA Convention and meet with the new state officers' team each year. This convention remains a highlight in my life. My passion for agriculture and involvement with the FFA has never waned.

I am thankful for the wonderful opportunities I have been given to serve others throughout my life; especially to help others achieve their potential. This has given me great happiness and contentment. I have now lived nearly one hundred years. Yet it seems only a short time. These thoughts caused me to once again write a book. With the assistance of my daughter Janice, in 2012 I completed a book that had been on my heart for many years, "Living Forever: Believing in what you cannot see." This small testimony book explains my journey into the spirit realm and back. The purpose of this book is to cause others to think deeply about their life and make wise decisions concerning their inevitable and eternal afterlife.

The longer I live, the more I realize the impact of attitudes on our lives. It is exciting we get to choose our attitude every day. I discovered youth is

Ray with his book, "Living Forever" in 2012

not a time of life or even an age; it is an attitude. No one grows old by merely living a number of years; people grow old by refusing to meet changes with excitement. I refuse to give up enthusiasm for life. Whether attending a state FFA convention or learning how to clog dance or hiking the Grand Canyon, I believe the key to happiness is living each moment to the fullest. Life without joy does not wrinkle our skin, it wrinkles our spirit. Worry, doubt, distrust, jealousy and despair; these are culprits that rob us of joy and good health, turning our spirits back to dust. My advice is to never dwell on negative words or events in life. A better decision is to focus on positive thoughts and actions.

Celebrating birthday number 99! Left to right; Mary Davison, Ray Hagan, Rev. Larry Griffin, Janice Wood, Jim Wood, Justin Weaver
March 2014

I am often asked to explain my longevity. I believe it is the Lord's decision how long we remain on Earth before we move to the spiritual realm. As long as we are allowed to live, we should encourage people to follow Him. Our words, actions and example need to direct others to Jesus. There is no retirement plan for a Christian. If He allows us to live, we should graciously serve Him. I leave this book looking forward to tomorrow and seeking the next opportunity to do good things for other people. I will continue to pray, aim high and stay focused.

Ray's Ways:

MY TOP TEN LIST FOR LIVING JOYFULLY TO ONE HUNDRED AND BEYOND...

1. Thank God constantly for all things, especially for looking after you.
2. Attend church regularly. Stay involved with God and His people.
3. Eat a variety of healthy foods, limiting fat, sugar, and fried foods.
4. Stay physically active. Dance. Walk. Enjoy nature.
5. Spend less than you earn. This reduces stress. Save money for emergencies. You will feel more secure and can help others in need.
6. Remain involved with people. Happiness comes from helping others.
7. Improve as you age. Eliminate bad habits. Start good habits.
8. Look for joy in all things, especially the hardest work.
9. Focus on others, not yourself. Help others achieve their potential.
10. Attitude is everything! Be adaptable. Life is change. Enjoy the ever-changing tide.

APPENDIX

1. Hagan Family Tree
2. Shirley Family Tree
3. Samuel Hagan Partition Petition *(Page One)*
4. Samuel Hagan Partition Petition *(Page Two)*
5. Robert & Sarah Hagan Family
6. Robert & Sarah Hagan Family
7. Wolf Hunt & Lincoln Barn
8. Samuel Shirley
9. William & Margaret Shirley Family
10. Ross & Pearle Hagan Family *(Early Years)*
11. Ross & Pearle Hagan Family
12. Ross Hagan's Barn Through The Years
13. Deeds to Ross Hagan Farm 1875
14. Deeds to Ross Hagan Farm 1912
15. Deeds to Ross Hagan Farm 1946
16. Bethel Church Through The Years
17. Bethel Church Cradle Roll Certificate
18. Raymond & Nita Hagan Family *(Early Years)*
19. Raymond Hagan Family
20. Raymond & Nita Hagan Family *(Grandchildren)*
21. Missouri Future Farmer Magazine 1984
22. Missouri Ruralist

HAGAN FAMILY

Samuel Hagan (1811-1851) & Elisabeth Heasley (1814-1896)

John Henry   Elizabeth   Sarah (Butler)   Robert W.
Angelina   Catherine   Belinda (Frank)   Jacob

Robert Wm. Hagan (1847-1928) & Sarah Taylor (1851 1923)

E. Jane (Dunn)
(1871-1936)

Frank Hagan
(1873-1909)

E. Rodell (Crawford)
(1874-1970)

Effie (Rockey)
(1876-1953)

Mirtis (Mark)
(1877-1962)

James Hagan
(1879-1964)

William Hagan
(1881-1949)

Infant Son Hagan
(1884-1884)

Ross Hagan
(1885-1968)

Fleety (Shirley)
(1887-1975)

Ernest Hagan
(1889-1978)

Gladys (Finney)
(1891-1966)

Coy Hagan
(1894-1966)

Ross Newton Hagan (1885-1968) &

Jessie (Lafollette)   Albert Ross   Raycel Shirley   Vee (Alley)
(1908-1927)   (1910-2009)   (1911-2003)   (1913-2002)

SHIRLEY FAMILY

Samuel Shirley (1837-1876) & Mahala Williams (1840-1911)

William R.   Erastus H.   Hattie (Weston)
Mary (Larason)   Raleigh Slover

William R. Shirley (1858-1943) & Margaret Slover (1858-1943)

Albert B. Shirley (1881-1907)
Minnie M. Shirley (1889-1889)
L. Blanche (Woods) (1882-1966)
Grace (Swingle) (1891-1985)
E. Pearle (Hagan) (1884-1966)
E. Gertrude Shirley (1894-1993)
Stella M. Shirley (1887-1888)
William G. Shirley (1899-1972)

Ethel "Pearle" Shirley (1884-1966)

Raymond Dale (1915-)   Reva (Cornett) (1916-2012)   William Darrell (1921-1969)

Raymond Hagan
March 7, 1942
V. Juanita Wharton

Partition Petition
Samuel Hagan Estate - May 1867
Farmington Township, Pennsylvannia

R & P

Rec'd Janry 4 1868
of Belinda E. Frank
per. C. Frank
One Hundred and
Twenty Three & 55/100
in full of costs of
this case
    Reid & Patrick
    Atty's for Ret's

same day, $10.00
refund to C. Frank
    Reid & Patrick

Rec'd Janry 4 1868
of Reid & Patrick,
$9.50, my fees in this
partition
    T.B.Barker Cl'k

Rec'd Janry 8 1868 of
Reid & Patrick $25.05
Twenty Five & o5/100
my costs:
    C.J.Rhea

In The Matter of The
Partition of the
Real Estate

NO 37 of

Samuel Hagan, late of
Farmington Township,
deseased.

At an Orphan's Court held at _____ in and for the County of Clarion on the fourth day of Febry AD1867 "Was presented the petition John H. Hagan, a son of Samu Hagan, late of the Township of Farmington in the said County, deceased. Respectfu presents that the said Samue Hagan died at about the (6th day of (Sept.) AD18 (51), intestate seized in his demise (not having made a v will) as of fee, of and in two certain messuages (a dwelling house with its out-buildings, gardens, etc or tracts of land situated in the said township of Farmington, bounded and described as follows, viz: One tract of land containing one hundred and thirty eight acres, more or less, bounded on th North by other lands formerly owned by said Sam Hagan, East by Hezikiah Shotts, South by lands Conrad Myers, West by lands of William Bell and Charles Leper, with the appurtenances. Also one other tract of land bounded on the North by Lot Slocum, East by land of Hezikiah Shotts, South the above described tract of land and West by t lot known as the John Laird Lot containing One Hundred Acres, with the appurtenances, and leav to to survive him:
A widow, Elizabeth Hagan and six children, viz: Joh H. Hagan, the petitioner, residing in Farmington to ship aforesaid, Elizabeth J. intermarried with Henr J. Shotts, residing in Elkhart County, Indiana, Sar A. intermarried with Ambrose Butler, residing in Venango County, Pennsylvania, Belinda E. intermarri with Christopher Frank, Robert W. Hagan and Jacob N. Hagan, both minor and having no guardians and residing in Farmington Township aforesaid.
    No partition of said real estate having been had, the petitioner prays the court to award an <u>Inquest</u> to make partition of the said Real Estate to and among the aforesaid parties according to their respectiv rights.

    And now TO WIT: Febry 4, 1867 <u>Inquest</u> awards personal notice on heirs residing in the county and by <u>publication</u> on the heirs residing out of the County.
                                              By The Court

    And now: Febry 20, 1867 Exc't Writ of Partition

    And now TO WIT: May 1867, Shff Rhea makes known that after having given due notice of the time of holding said <u>Inquest</u> he did on the 26th day of March, 1867, go upon the premises, taking with him twelve good and lawful men of his bailiwick, The said <u>Inquest</u> on their solemn oaths and affirmations say that the property cannot be divided without prejudice to or spoiling the whole and havevalued and apprais the same as follows: Property No 1, at twenty one hundred dollars ($2100.00) and Property NO 2, at six hundred dollars ($600.00)
                                                    Shff Rhea $11.55
                                                    Printer 3.00

    And now TO WIT: May 6, 1867 <u>Inquest</u> confirms "

And now, May 9, 1867, Inquest confirmer absolutely and it is decreed that the same be and remain firm and stable forever. And rule on the heirs to accept or refuse awards.

By The Court

And now TO WIT: May 16, 1867, Rule on the heris to accept or refuse

And now TO WIT: Sept. 2 1867, Shff Rhea makes return: "Served the within notice on Elizabeth Hagan; Belinda E. Frank and Christopher H. Frank, Guardian, personally, who severally accepted service there- and on John H. Hagan, Elizabeth J. Shotts and Sarah A. Butler by Publication in the Clarin (Clarion) Democrat for three successive times

C.J.Rhea, Shff,   P'nt $2.50

And now TO WIT: Sept. 5, 1867, Heirs called in open court and property awarded to Belinda E. Frank at the appraised value of the same being $2700.00

SCHEDULE OF DISTRIBUTION
```
    Amount of appraisal              $2700.00
    Deduct am't of costs of Partition
    Viz: Attys Reid & Patrick    $90.00
         Shff Rhea                18.55
          "    "  printing         5.50
         T. B. Barker, clk of ct   9.50
                                 $123.55
                                          $2576.45
    Life Estate set apart for
      the use of the widow
         Elizabeth Hagan         $858.82
    to John H. Hagan              286.27
         Elizabeth J. Shotts      286.27
         Sarah A. Butler          286.27
         Belinda E. Frank         286.27
         Robert W. Hagan          286.27
         Jacob N. Hagan           286.27
                                $1717.63
         $2,576.45
```

The widow's share, Eight Hundred and Fifty Eight 82/100 Dollars to be distributed at her death among the heirs, will be to each heir the sum of One Hundred and Forty Three 73/100 Dollars.

Robert William & Sarah (Taylor) Hagan
Established 1870

Robert & Sarah's "Weaning Farm" house - 1911
Pictured from Right: Pearle, Jessie, Baby Albert, and Ross Hagan

The Robert & Sarah (Taylor) Hagan Family

Front Row:
Ross Hagan • Robert Hagan • Sarah Taylor Hagan • James Hagan • Ernest Hagan

Middle Row:
Jane Hagan Dunn • Eff Hagan Rocky • Coy Hagan • William Hagan • Gladys Hagan Finney

Back Row:
Fleeta May Hagan Shirley • Dell Hagan Crawford • Mirt Hagan Marget

Children of Robert Wm Hagan (1847 -1928) & Sarah Taylor Hagan (1851 -1923)

Eliza Jane Hagan Dunn (1871 - 1936)*
Frank Emory Hagan (1873 - 1909)*
Elizabeth Rodell Hagan Crawford (1874 - 1970)*
Effie May Hagan Rockey (1876 - 1953)*
Mirtis Loretta Hagan Mark (1877 - 1962)*
James Stuart Hagan (1879 - 1964)*
William Taylor Hagan (1881 - 1949)*
Infant Son Hagan (1884 - 1884)*
Ross Newton Hagan (1885 - 1968)
Fleety Beatrice Hagan Shirley (1887 - 1975)*
Ernest Clarence Hagan (1889 - 1978)*
Gladys Irma Hagan Finney (1891 - 1966)*
Coy Virgil Hagan (1894 - 1966)*

Will Hagan: Son of Robert and Sarah Hagan

Wolf hunt in Watonga, Oklahoma. Will Hagan is located on the left side, back row near the carcasses of three wolves. He wrote on the picture, "wolves killed west of Watonga, Okla, Jan 1915" This picture was enclosed in a letter from Will Hagan, to my dad Ross Hagan. Will was living on a farm in Oklahoma he homesteaded in 1907.

Lincoln Barn on the Robert Hagan Farm

Presidential Elections were held in this barn in November of 1860 when Abraham Lincoln was elected President of the United States.

Samuel Shirley
Honorable Discharge from Union Army (Civil War)
May 15, 1865

(Ray Hagan's Great-Grandfather)

William R & Margaret *(Slover)* Shirley Family
Established February 22, 1880

Albert Bertam Shirley (1881 - 1907)
Lillian Blanche Shirley Woods (1882 - 1966)
Ethel Pearle Shirley Hagan (1884 - 1966)
Stella Maude Shirley (1887 - 1888)

Children

Minnie May Shirley (1889 - 1889)
Grace Edith Shirley Swingle (1891 - 1985)
Elsie Gertrude Shirley (1894 - 1993)
William Glenn Shirley (1899 - 1972)

Ray's Grandparents:

Ethel Pearle Shirley
- 3 years -

Ethel Pearle Shirley
- Around 1906 -

Nita & Ray Hagan, Margaret Shirley
- 1942 -

Ross & Pearle (Shirley) Hagan Family
Established 1907

Front Row: Ross and E. Pearle
Back Row: Raymond, Vee (Alley), Albert, Reva (Cornett), Raycel, Darrell

Barn designed and built by Ross Hagan in 1915

Selected as the "Most Beautiful Barn in America" in 2007 by "Country Life" magazine because it showcases the beauty and heritage of rural America.

Warranty Deed
George & Martha Dunn sold farm to Jacob Hagan
for $440 on June 27, 1875

WARRANTY DEED

Geo. D. Barnard & Co., St. Louis

This Indenture, Made on the 21st day of June A. D. One Thousand Eight Hundred and Seventy Five by and between George G. Dunn and Martha A. Dunn his wife of Mercer County, State of Missouri, part us of the first part, and Jacob Hagan of the County of Mercer, in the State of Missouri, part y of the second part: WITNESSETH, That the said part us of the first part, in consideration of the sum of Four Hundred and Forty DOLLARS to them paid by the said part y of the second part, the receipt of which is hereby acknowledged, do by these presents, Grant, Bargain and Sell, Convey and Confirm unto the said part y of the second part, his heirs and assigns, the following described lots, tracts, or parcels of land lying, being and situate in the County of Mercer, and State of Missouri, to-wit:

All the East half of the North West quarter of Section No. (12) Twelve, Township No. (66) Sixty Six, Range No. (25) Twenty Five.

TO HAVE AND TO HOLD the premises aforesaid, with all and singular the rights, privileges, appurtenances and immunities thereto belonging, or in anywise appertaining, unto the said part y of the second part, and unto his heirs and assigns forever; the said George Dunn and Martha A. Dunn his wife hereby covenanting that they are lawfully seized of an indefeasible estate in fee in the premises herein conveyed; that they have good right to convey the same; that the said premises are free and clear of any incumbrances done or suffered by them or those under whom they claim; and that they will Warrant and Defend the title to the said premises unto the said part y of the second part, and unto his heirs and assigns forever against the lawful claims and demands of all persons whomsoever.

IN WITNESS WHEREOF, The said part us of the first part ha ve hereunto set their hands and seals the day and year first above written.

Signed, Sealed and Delivered in Presence of us:

George G. Dunn [Seal]
[Seal]
Martha A. Dunn [Seal]
[Seal]

STATE OF MISSOURI, } ss.
County of Mercer

BE IT REMEMBERED, That on this 21st day of June A. D. 1875, before the undersigned, a Justice of the Peace within and for the County of Mercer George G. Dunn and Martha A. Dunn his wife who are personally known to me to be the same persons whose names are subscribed to the foregoing instrument of writing as parties thereto, and acknowledged the same to be their act and deed for the purposes therein mentioned. And the said Martha A. Dunn his wife being by me first made acquainted with the contents of said instrument, upon an examination separate and apart from her said husband, acknowledged that she executed the same, and relinquished her dower in the Real Estate therein mentioned, freely and without fear, compulsion or undue influence of her said husband.

IN TESTIMONY WHEREOF, I have hereunto set my hand and affixed my official seal, at my office in Lindley Township, the day and year first above written.

My term of office as a Notary Public will expire

M. G. Maxwell Justice of the Peace

STATE OF MISSOURI, } ss.
County of

BE IT REMEMBERED, That on this day of A. D. 18 , before the undersigned, a within and for the County of aforesaid, personally came who is personally known to me to be the same person whose name is subscribed to the foregoing instrument of writing as a party thereto, and acknowledged the same to be act and deed for the purposes therein mentioned. And the said further declared to be single and unmarried.

IN TESTIMONY WHEREOF, I have hereunto set my hand and affixed my official seal, at my office in the day and year first above written.

My term of office as a Notary Public will expire

Filed for Record the 7th day of March A. D. 1878, at 1 o'clock minutes P. M.
By Deputy. Wm. M. Casteel Recorder.

Book 2 Page 564

Warranty Deed

Jacob & Hira Hagan sold farm to Ross Hagan for **$12,265** on January 18, 1912

Book 67, Page 635

This Indenture, Made on the 18th day of January A.D. twelve by and between Jacob N. Hagan and Hira his wife of Wayne County, Iowa

of the ___ ___ Ross Hagan

of the County of Mercer in the State of Missouri part of the Second Part:

WITNESSETH, That the said parties of the First Part, in consideration of the sum of Twelve thousand two hundred sixty-five $12,265.00 to be paid by the said part of the Second Part, the receipt of which is hereby acknowledged, do by these presents, GRANT, etc.

SELL, CONVEY AND CONFIRM, unto the said part of the Second Part his heirs and assigns, the following described Lots, Tracts or Land, lying, being and situated in the County of Mercer and State of Missouri, to-wit:

The Northwest Quarter of Section Twelve (12) also the Southwest Quarter of the North East Quarter and twenty three and one half acre being all of the northwest quarter of the north east quarter of Section 12, lying south of the public road township 66 Range 25

[Signatures:]
Jacob N. Hagan [SEAL]
Hira C. Hagan [SEAL]

State of Iowa
County of Wayne

On this 18th day of January A.D. 1912, before me personally appeared Jacob N. Hagan and Hira C. Hagan

his wife, to me known to be the persons described in and who executed the foregoing instrument, and acknowledged that they executed the same as their free act and deed.

IN TESTIMONY WHEREOF, I have hereunto set my hand and affixed my official seal, at my office in Lineville, Iowa the day and year first above written.

My term expires July 4th 1912.

E. L. Calbreath, Notary Public

The foregoing Deed was filed for Record in this office on the 7 day of March A.D. 1912

Warranty Deed

Ross & Pearle Hagan sold farm to Raycel and Ruby Hagan for **$15,000** on December 4, 1946

Book 99, Page 644

WARRANTY DEED, with Statutory Acknowledgments.

This Indenture, Made on the 4th day of December A.D. One Thousand Nine Hundred and Forty Six by and between Ross H. Hagan and Ethel P. Hagan of the County of Mercer in the State of Missouri part_ies_ of the first part, and Raycel L. Hagan and Ruby L. Hagan, husband and wife of the County of Mercer in the State of Missouri part_ies_ of the second part,

WITNESSETH, That the said part_y_ of the first part, in consideration of the sum of Fifteen Thousand dollars ($15000.00) DOLLARS, to them paid by the said part_ies_ of the second part, the receipt of which is hereby acknowledged, do by these presents Grant, Bargain and Sell, Convey and Confirm unto the said part_ies_ of the second part, their heirs and assigns, the following described lots, tracts or parcels of land lying, being and situate in the County of Mercer and State of Missouri, to-wit: All

The southwest quarter of the northeast quarter and the whole of the northwest quarter of section twelve, in township sixty six north of range twenty five west.
Also all that part of the northwest quarter of the northeast quarter of said section twelve lying south of the road, containing twenty three and one half acres more or less.
The premises hereby conveyed contain in the aggregate two hundred twenty three and one half acres, more or less, subject to easement for public highways.

$16.50 Internal revenue stamps affixed and cancelled

TO HAVE AND TO HOLD, The premises aforesaid, with all and singular the rights, privileges, appurtenances and immunities thereto belonging or in anywise appertaining, unto the said part_ies_ of the second part, and unto _____ heirs and assigns, forever; the said Ross H. Hagan and Ethel P. Hagan hereby covenanting that they are lawfully seized of an indefeasible estate in fee in the premises herein conveyed; that they have good right to convey the same; that the said premises are free and clear of any incumbrances done or suffered by them or those under whom they claim, and that they will Warrant and Defend the title to the said premises unto the said part_ies_ of the second part, and unto their heirs and assigns forever, against the lawful claims and demands of all persons whomsoever.

IN WITNESS WHEREOF, The said part_ies_ of the first part ha_ve_ hereunto set their hand_s_ and seal_s_, the day and year first above written.

Signed, Sealed and Delivered in Presence of Us:

Ross H. Hagan [Seal]
Ethel P. Hagan [Seal]

STATE OF MISSOURI,
County of Mercer ss. ON THIS 4th day of December 1946, before me personally appeared Ross H. Hagan and Ethel P. Hagan his wife, to me known to be the persons described in and who executed the foregoing instrument, and acknowledged that they executed the same as their free act and deed.
IN TESTIMONY WHEREOF, I have hereunto set my hand and affixed my official seal, at my office in Princeton, Mo. the day and year first above written.
[Seal]
My term expires March 9th, 1949   Hubert Fuller Notary Public.

STATE OF MISSOURI,
County of _____ ss. ON THIS ____ day of _____ 19__ before me personally appeared _____
to me known to be the person_ described in and who executed the foregoing instrument, and acknowledged that ___ executed the same as ___ free act and deed.
And the said _____ further declared _____ to be single and unmarried.
IN TESTIMONY WHEREOF, I have hereunto set my hand and affixed my official seal, at my office in _____
the day and year first above written.
My term expires _____, 19__ _____ Notary Public.

The foregoing Deed was filed for record in this office on the 5th day of Dec A.D. 1946 at 2 o'clock 15 minutes P.M.
By Mabel Morris Deputy Orel Fuley Recorder.
REMARKS:

Bethel Church
Established 1856

This is to certify that on this fourth day of May 1880, I dedicated to God by Baptism four children of Robert Wm & Sarah Martha Hague of Mercer Co. Mo. named and dedicated as follows:
Elisabeth Rodell, born Oct. 30th 1874,
Ellie May, born May 6th 1876,
Mirtie Terette, born Aug. 26th 1877,
and James Stuart, born Oct. 6th 1879.
Wm Taylor
of the South India Conference
May 4th 1880.

This is to Certify

That Raymond Dale Hagan,

Born _____ has been admitted to

The Cradle Roll Department

of the _Bethel M.E._ Sunday School.

Enrolled Oct 26 1917 W. A. Yetter, Pastor.

W. L. Hallcroft, Superintendent.   Nell Crasford, Superintendent of Cradle Roll Department.

THE METHODIST BOOK CONCERN   NEW YORK—CINCINNATI

Raymond & Nita (Wharton) Hagan Family
Established 1942

March Bride

Photo by Lass-Truitt.
Mrs. Raymond Hagan, who was married to Mr. Hagan on March 7 at Liberty. She is the former Miss Juanita Wharton, daughter of Mr. and Mrs. L. H. Wharton of LaMonte.

Sharon Juanita

Jane Marie

Janice Elaine

Raymond Hagan Family

Sharon Juanita

Jane Marie

Janice Elaine

Back Row: Sharon, Ray, Janice
Seated: Jane and Kay

Raymond & Nita (Wharton) Hagan Family

Grandchildren

Jeffery Allen

Patricia Marie

Great-Grandchildren

LeeAnna Marie

Austin Dale

Great-Great Grandchildren

Chase Alexander

Sierra Rose

Gemma Marie

Missouri Future Farmer

VOLUME XLVIII SEPTEMBER-OCTOBER, 1984

RAYMOND D. HAGAN

State Executive Secretary For the Missouri Association FFA Retires

Mr. Raymond D. Hagan is retiring as Executive Secretary of this Missouri Association of FFA on November 30, 1984.

For the past 44 years he has shared his knowledge with thousands of FFA members in Missouri and has been instrumental in developing competent agricultural leadership. Mr. Hagan's dedication to the FFA has been strong since the time, as a greenhand, he served the Princeton FFA Chapter as "watch dog" (sentinal). He later became a vocational agriculture instructor and served the Green Ridge, Cainsville, and Princeton chapters as advisor.

Following seven years of teaching he became District Supervisor of Agricultural Education for the Department of Elementary and Secondary Education, where he has completed 36 years. During the past 29 years he has also served as Executive Secretary, Missouri Association FFA. Other duties have included many years of service as livestock superintendent at the American Royal and FFA superintendent at the Missouri State Fair.

After directing 29 state FFA officer teams and being "father" to 428 state officers it is evident that Mr. Hagan's experience as Princeton's "watch dog" has proven very beneficial. He has seen 11 of his state officers attain national office, and his guidance was integral to the development of such leaders as Jerry Litton, Terry Heiman, James Boillot and Larry Case. His achievements have meen recognized on all levels through his reception of both the Honorary State and Honorary American Farmer degrees.

Mr. Hagan has been a fundamental and driving force behind vocational agriculture and FFA in Missouri and the Nation. We wish him well upon his retirement.

FFA History Book
written by Raymond Hagan
in 1978

MISSOURI RURALIST

FEBRUARY 23, 1985 — ONE DOLLAR

Raymond Hagan, FFA leader retires

CPSIA information can be obtained at www.ICGtesting.com
Printed in the USA
LVOW03*0358120115

422445LV00021B/124/P